W9-BNF-479

Unmatched Power
Unmet Principles
The Human Rights Dimensions of US Training of Foreign Military and Police Forces

Cover: Johor, Malaysia—U.S. Marines and Malaysian soldiers participate in a simulated amphibious assault during the seventh annual Cooperation Afloat Readiness and Training 2001 exercise July 24. CARAT exercises employ simulated military scenarios designed to prepare U.S. and Malaysian forces to meet future challenges of disaster relief and humanitarian aid. CARAT, a series of bilateral exercises, takes place throughout the Western Pacific each summer. It aims to increase regional cooperation and promote interoperability with each country. The countries participating in CARAT 01 were: Indonesia, Singapore, Philippines, Thailand, Malaysia and Brunei. (U.S. Navy photo by Photographer's Mate 2nd Class Erin A. Zocco)

Amnesty International is a worldwide human rights activist movement with more than 1.1 million members in over 140 countries and territories, including nearly 300,000 members in the United States.

Amnesty International's vision is of a world in which every person enjoys all of the human rights enshrined in the Universal Declaration of Human Rights and other international human rights standards.

Amnesty International undertakes research and action focused on preventing and ending grave abuses of the rights to physical and mental integrity, freedom of conscience and expression, and freedom from discrimination, within the context of its work to promote all human rights.

Amnesty International is independent of any government, political ideology, or religious creed. It does not support or oppose any government or political system. It is concerned solely with the impartial protection of human rights.

Amnesty International is funded largely by its worldwide membership and by donations from the public.

Unmatched Power
Unmet Principles
The Human Rights Dimensions of US Training of Foreign Military and Police Forces

Amnesty International USA Publications

First published in 2002 by
Amnesty International USA
322 Eighth Avenue
New York, NY 10001

www.amnestyusa.org

© Copyright
Amnesty International USA Publications 2002
ISBN: 1-887204-34-2
Original language: English

Printed by:
Globe Litho
One Teaneck Road
Ridgefield, NJ 07660

All rights reserved. No part of this
publication may be reproduced, stored in
a retrieval system, or transmitted, in any
form or by any means, electronic,
mechanical, photocopying, recording
and/or otherwise without the prior
permission of the publishers.

CONTENTS

EXECUTIVE SUMMARY   vii

1 INTRODUCTION: CHANGE AND CONTINUITY   1

2 OVERVIEW OF US FOREIGN MILITARY AND POLICE   7
TRAINING PROGRAMS AND INSTITUTIONS

3 HUMAN RIGHTS TRAINING AND THE US GOVERNMENT   30

4 PRIORITY AREAS FOR ACTION   63

APPENDIX 1   70

APPENDIX 2   76

ENDNOTES   78

Executive summary

US training of foreign military and police forces: the human rights dimensions

The United States government now trains at least 100,000 foreign police and soldiers from more than 150 countries each year in US military and policing doctrine and methods, as well as war-fighting skills. These numbers have increased markedly since September 11th, 2001, with intensified operations in countries including Afghanistan, Georgia, the Philippines, and Yemen. Most of these deployments are considered "anti-terrorism" training of foreign forces, but such US training is not unique to the post-September 11th environment.

Today's US military training can have unanticipated consequences tomorrow

Military training is a long-term benefit, and the skills gained through training can be transferred easily from one military or police unit to another. US training offered to other nations should, therefore, be a carefully considered element of US foreign policy, conducted with oversight, transparency, accountability and appropriate guidance. The importance of these checks and balances is underscored by the record of US training in places such as Colombia, Indonesia and Rwanda, where military forces have committed human rights violations in the context of armed conflict.

Throughout the decade of the 1990s, the record of one US military training institution, in particular, attracted public scrutiny in the United States. The US Army's School of the Americas offered training and education to Latin American soldiers, some of whom went on to commit human rights violations, including the 1989 murder in El Salvador of six Jesuit priests, their housekeeper and her daughter. Then, in 1996, it came to light that, in the 1980s and early 1990s, the School of the Americas had used manuals that advocated practices such as torture, extortion, kidnapping and execution.

These revelations largely were the result of a concerted campaign to discover and disclose the record of the school and its alumni by nongovernmental organizations, including the School of the Americas Watch. This campaign generated tremendous pressure for reform throughout the 1990s, and today the School of the Americas has a new name, a new charter, and a significantly different curriculum, which includes coursework in human rights and humanitarian law. Nonetheless, the US government has never held anyone accountable for the training manuals or the behavior of graduates of the School of the Americas, and many critics continue to call for the closure of this institution.

The vast network of US training operations

The School of the Americas (or the Western Hemisphere Institute for Security Cooperation, as it is now known) is, however, only one small part of a vast and complex network of US programs for training foreign military and police forces. Some of this education and training is conducted in the United States, funded either by the foreign government itself or with US loans and grants. In addition to the Western Hemisphere Institute for Security Cooperation, there are approximately 275 military schools and installations in the United States, offering over 4,100 courses. Tens of thousands of students train in these programs, but far more receive some US training in their own nations through a variety of programs, including military exercises.

The United States also provides training to foreign police forces through a range of programs, including those overseen by the Departments of Justice and State and the Federal Bureau of Investigation.

In addition, US private commercial contractors conduct training of both foreign militaries and foreign police forces. In some cases, the US Departments of Defense, Justice and State hire private companies to implement government-designed training programs; in others, foreign governments directly hire private US companies.

Imperatives of oversight and human rights training

A number of laws govern US training of foreign forces, including the Arms Export Control Act, the Foreign Assistance Act and an amendment to the annual Foreign Operations and Defense Appropriations Acts known as the "Leahy Law." The Leahy Law, first introduced in 1996, requires background screening for past human rights violations of foreign recipients of US military and police training. Although the US Departments of State and Defense have made progress in implementing the Leahy Law, there is still no standardized process for conducting such background screenings.

In practice, the quality of the background vetting varies from US Embassy to US Embassy, depending on such factors as the level of effort of embassy staff and the amount of information available about prospective students' backgrounds. Moreover, the screening requirement does not extend to training purchased by foreign governments with their own funds, which accounts for the majority of US training of foreign troops. Follow-up assessment of international military students who have received training from the US also is limited.

In addition to this legal framework, some US military training includes human rights content, although there is no systematic requirement for such content in the majority of US training and education provided to foreign forces. Two programs that routinely feature such content are the Western Hemisphere Institute for Security Cooperation (WHINSEC), which features a mandatory human rights course, and International Military Education and Training (IMET), which includes courses on civil-military relations, human rights and military justice. In contrast, there is no mandated requirement for human rights instruction in the training of foreign law enforcement officials. With the exception of a few programs, information on whether police training includes human rights content is not publicly available.

The United States also provides operational training to foreign forces, often through military exercises. Most of these exercises do not include any kind of screening for human rights abuses or human rights and humanitarian law content. The exception is Joint Combined Exchange Training (JCET), a program that allows US Special Operations Forces to exercise with foreign forces. The JCET program requires background screening of all foreign participants.

Case studies: Rwanda, Indonesia, Colombia

Operational training, in particular, tends to take place with little foreign policy oversight and accountability. The risks of such circumstances are underscored by case studies from Rwanda, Indonesia and Colombia. The Rwandan Patriotic Army has been implicated in widespread human rights violations, including the "disappearance" and killing of unarmed civilians. Although it remains unclear exactly which units were trained, US Special Forces did provide lethal, combat training to elements of the Rwandan Patriotic Army before these violations took place. US forces continued to provide lethal training to Indonesian soldiers after the 1991 killings of unarmed demonstrators in East Timor—and in spite of a ban from the US Congress on military training of Indonesian forces. In Colombia, US forces continue to provide military training, despite widespread human rights abuses by both the Colombian military forces and the paramilitary forces linked to them.

Amnesty International's recommendations to the US government

Based on this report, Amnesty International recommends that the US government take the following steps:

- Increase the transparency and accountability of the training provided to foreign militaries. In particular, the US government needs to increase the scrutiny of training provided by private US contractors and enact the Human Rights Information Act and Foreign Military Training Responsibility Act to enable greater disclosure of past training and to address current oversight, accountability and transparency shortfalls.

- Mainstream human rights and humanitarian law education into all foreign military training; increase the transparency and accountability of the training provided to foreign militaries.

- Strengthen background vetting of all foreign trainees, including those whose governments purchase training or who receive training from private contractors.

- Develop a more coordinated system for allocating military, security and police training to foreign governments.

- Provide oversight of and policy guidance for the use of US Special Operations Forces (SOF) for training of foreign forces, especially training involving regular (conventional) forces.

- Establish an independent commission to investigate the past activities of the School of the America and its graduates, particularly the use of training manuals that advocated torture and other illegal activities. Pending the publication of the findings of the commission, training at the Western Hemisphere Institute for Security Cooperation (the institution that succeeded the School of the Americas in 2001) should be suspended.

1
Introduction: change and continuity

"Training includes formal or informal instruction of foreign students in the United States or overseas by officers or employees of the United States, contract technicians, or contractors (including instruction at civilian institutions), or by correspondence courses, technical, education, or information publications and media of all kinds, training aid, orientation, training exercise, and military advice to foreign military units and forces."
—US Arms Export Control Act of 1976, Section 47

On March 12, 1995, armed soldiers rampaged through the Karte Seh district of Kabul, Afghanistan, killing and beating unarmed civilians and raping women. A few years later, similar atrocities would again take place. The difference was the perpetrators: the first time, it was the forces of the Northern Alliance and the second, the Taliban.

The Northern Alliance and the Taliban have become names familiar to most of the world, but these fighters have a shared past, as well. Many in the military leadership of both groups fought together during the war of resistance against Soviet occupation as so-called Mujahideen fighters.

> "They shot my father right in front of me. He was a shopkeeper. It was nine o'clock at night. They came to our house and told him they had orders to kill him because he allowed me to go to school. The Mujahideen had already stopped me from going to school, but that was not enough. They then came and killed my father. I cannot describe what they did to me after killing my father . . ."[1]

The Mujahideen received substantial assistance in the form of money, weapons and training from the United States and other foreign powers during the Soviet occupation of Afghanistan.[2] Some of the largest and best-equipped Mujahideen factions that were supported by the United States were made up of Islamist extremists, the most prominent being Gulbuddin Hekmatyar.[3] Hekmatyar, the leader of Hezb-e Islami (Party of Islam) and Afghanistan's Prime Minister from 1992 to 1995, cooperated with other Mujahideen during the resistance against the Soviets.[4] Hezb-e Islami was responsible for widespread human rights violations, including deadly attacks on journalists and other civilians, abductions, torture and rape.[5] Despite this dire record and protests by Members of Congress, the United States government continued to offer material support for Hekmatyar in the 1990s.[6]

US training of the mujahideen in Afghanistan offers a cautionary tale. Military training is a commodity, one that is transferred easily from one military unit to another. Troops trained today for one specific use will still be trained in the future, when circumstances differ, and can pass on their skills to other units that may have missions the trainer would not support. Therefore, military training should be reconciled with the overall political-military context and the human rights realities on the ground. Training of foreign militaries should be a carefully considered element of a nation's foreign policy, conducted with oversight, transparency and accountability.

Yet the training of foreign military, security and police officials and armed groups remains an important feature of United States national security policy that is conducted with little oversight or concerted guidance. The Department of State's budget alone for FY 2003 requests $3.6 billion under foreign assistance, which encompasses a variety of programs that provide security assistance, military equipment and training.[7] The United States government trains as many as 100,000 foreign police and soldiers from more than 150 countries[8] in US military doctrine and methods, as well as war-fighting skills. Moreover, these numbers have increased markedly since September 11, 2001.

Long before the attacks on the World Trade Center and Pentagon in September 2001 added more urgency to United States security policy, the United States was increasing its training of foreign militaries and law enforcement officials. Following the end of the Cold War, the United States drastically reduced direct military assistance to most nations, often compensating with an increase in relatively inexpensive training programs.

The expansion in training programs also reflects broader missions for the US military and law enforcement officials, including counter-narcotics trafficking, counter-terrorism and promotion of local or regional peacekeeping forces. Finally, training with foreign military forces is a prime component of the US government's National Defense Strategy, which calls for US forces to train and operate with other countries, including participating in joint and combined training and "experimentation."[9]

Table 1
Post-September 11 International Military Training Activities

Country	Military assistance funding[10]	Description and justification for increased cooperation
Philippines	$22.4 million	US forces are currently training 4,000 to 5,000 Filipino soldiers, mostly on Basilan island. There are approximately 660 US troops present, including 160 Special Operations Forces. This training was undertaken to improve the Philippine military's "anti-terrorism capability," in particular against the armed group Abu Sayyaf.[11]
Yemen	$2.65 million	Two dozen US military advisors are already present in Yemen, with teams of additional advisors to arrive soon. Vice President Cheney visited on March 14, 2002 to discuss a US program for training Yemeni military and police, while Ali Abdallah Salih, president of Yemen, seeks funds to develop a coast guard and acquire military equipment from the United States. The US Administration has expressed concerns about al-Qaida's influence in Yemen.[12]
Republic of Georgia	$8.2 million	President Bush announced that the United States would send 150 military trainers to Georgia, with a training program allocation of $64 million.[13] The US Administration believes that al-Qaida affiliates are operating in the Pankiski Gorge near the Russian border.[14]

In theory, such programs could facilitate the development of well-trained, more professional forces that are better equipped to protect the stability of nations and the security of civilians. In practice, however, the US government often provides training or equipment to security forces regardless of their conduct, even when that conduct includes human rights abuses. For example, US forces provided combat training to Indonesian forces directly responsible for widespread human rights violations in Indonesia and East Timor; Rwandan Patriotic Army troops implicated in widespread extra-judicial executions; and Colombian army units implicated in killings by paramilitary forces. Today, US forces exercise and train alongside security and police forces from Egypt, El Salvador, India, Pakistan, Saudi Arabia, Sri Lanka, Turkey, and many other nations whose

Linking military training with human rights abuses

On the morning of November 16, 1989, Salvadoran soldiers made their way into the Pastoral Center at the Central American University in San Salvador. They ordered five Jesuit priests to go outside and lie face down on the ground, where they were subsequently shot and killed. A sixth priest, the housekeeper and her 16-year-old daughter were then murdered inside the residence. The Jesuits had been labeled "subversives" by the Salvadoran government for speaking out against the socioeconomic structure of Salvadoran society.[15]

Of the twenty-six soldiers subsequently implicated in the murders of the Jesuit priests and women in El Salvador, nineteen had received training at the School of the Americas. Three officers had received some human rights training while at the school. Additionally, one soldier had attended the Special Forces Officer Course at Ft. Bragg in late 1988 and early 1989.

The battalion to which these soldiers belonged was being trained by US Army Special Forces in El Salvador in the days before and after the murders.[16] (See section 3.3.3 for a more detailed history of the School of the Americas.)

Techniques advocated in SOA training manuals, 1982–1991:[17]

- Motivation by fear
- Payment of bounties for enemy dead
- False imprisonment
- Use of truth serum
- Torture
- Execution
- Extortion
- Kidnapping and arresting a target's family members

militaries and other security forces have been implicated in human rights abuses.

With some exceptions, public knowledge and official oversight of the vast and murky network of foreign military training programs continues to be minimal. The Department of Defense, the Department of State, and the Department of Justice support over a dozen distinct programs spread throughout several government agencies and involving some 275 US facilities. The training infrastructure is far-flung and complex, including several funding mechanisms, multiple legislative authorizations, and numerous bureaucratic programs and institutions. In addition, the 1990s saw a boom in the US government's use and licensing of private military contractors to provide training for foreign security forces. The CIA's Directorate of Operations also runs covert training operations, about which very little is publicly known.

One relatively small part of this training system—the US Army's School of the Americas (SOA)[18]—has received considerable public scrutiny in the United States. In 1989, Salvadoran soldiers who had trained at SOA were implicated in the murder of a woman, her teenage daughter and six Jesuit priests, spawning greater public awareness, a wave of protests against the school, and calls for the closure of SOA.

The SOA's critics argue that human rights abuses perpetrated by its alumni are either a direct result of the training they received while at SOA or that SOA has done little to discourage abusive practices or establish accountability for past practices. As evidence, they point to seven training manuals used by SOA from 1982 to 1991 that advocate practices inconsistent with US and international law and stated Pentagon policies.

Under pressure, the US Army "closed" the School of the Americas, reopening it in January 2001 as the Western Hemisphere Institute for Security Cooperation. The Army changed the school's charter and codified some already existing oversight structures. (This report subsequently refers to the current institution as WHINSEC-SOA and to the institution before 2001 as SOA.) Although the campaign to close WHINSEC-SOA continues unabated, the public outcry also led the US Congress to require that WHINSEC-SOA provide more human rights awareness training for military students than any other US training facility.[19]

In addition to the public storm surrounding WHINSEC-SOA, pressure for reform from Congress, private organizations, and the media led to some changes in American training of foreign military and police throughout the 1990s and in 2000. This study examines the nature and effectiveness of those reforms and identifies the relationship between human rights and US military training of foreign security forces.

Chapter 2 charts the known universe of military and police training programs. Chapter 3 assesses efforts by the US military to advance human rights and civil-military relations through these programs, including WHINSEC-School of the Americas. Chapter 3 also presents three case studies of recent and ongoing military training relationships where human rights violations have occurred or continue to occur. Chapter 4 offers Amnesty International USA's recommendations.

2
Overview of US foreign military and police training programs and institutions

"There is no comparable historical example of so many diverse sovereign states . . . entrusting so many potential national leaders to the education and training of another state. While other countries such as France, the United Kingdom, Germany, Israel, Taiwan and Canada have offered similar forms of security assistance, and still do, the global scale undertaken by the United States continues to be unprecedented."

—John A. Cope (USA, ret.), *International Military Education and Training: An Assessment,* 1995

To understand the effects of American education and training on human rights around the world, it is helpful to have a sense of the scope of such training and education and to whom it is made available.

This chapter profiles the vast universe of programs, institutions, and mechanisms that the United States government uses to educate or train foreign military, police and security forces. Many of these programs, such as International Military Education and Training (IMET—see section 2.1.1), Joint Combined Exchange Training (JCET—see section 2.2.1), and private military contractor training (see section 2.5), have been directly or indirectly tied to foreign forces implicated in human rights violations.[20]

There is no single US government entity charged with providing or overseeing military education and training for US troops or for the foreign troops trained by US uniformed personnel.[21] A recent Department of Defense report chronicled this lack of oversight and labeled military training "something slapped together ad hoc."[22]

Within the US Department of State and the US Department of Defense, multiple agencies and offices are involved in training and education programs. There are currently guidelines in place for screening potential candidates for many military training programs for past human rights abuses. Nonetheless, there does not appear to be a clearly delineated or consistent system for deciding which nations receive training, what kind of training will be offered, where the training will be provided, exactly how candidates will be screened for past human rights violations, or how training program alumni will be tracked.

In addition, intelligence and other government agencies may provide some training to military personnel. Private contractors also train foreign forces—sometimes at the request of the US government and other times independently. These programs

Deciphering military terminology

Tactics: How units are used in combat; the ordered arrangement and maneuver of units in relation to each other and/or the adversary.

Doctrine: Fundamental principles that guide all military action, usually informed by national objectives or policy. Although doctrine is authoritative, it tends to require judgment in application.

Operational training: Training that develops, maintains, or improves the immediate ability of individuals or units to play their role in combat or other military operations.

Unconventional warfare: A broad spectrum of military and paramilitary operations conducted in enemy-held, enemy-controlled or politically sensitive territory, including guerrilla war, evasion and escape, subversion, sabotage and other covert operations. This type of warfare may use predominantly indigenous personnel with support and direction coming from an external source during all conditions of war or peace.

Psychological operations: Activities in peace and war that influence the attitudes and behavior of neutral, friendly or hostile audiences in order to achieve political and military objectives.[23]

may be offered without any oversight or consistent process for allocating such training.

Training of police and other law enforcement officials is even more dispersed throughout the US government, with programs funded through a number of different budgets in a convoluted manner and administered through multiple offices at the Departments of Defense, Justice, State, Treasury and Transportation.[24] Although the Bureau of International Narcotics and Law Enforcement at the State Department is responsible for coordinating all police training programs, the General Accounting Office of the US Congress has acknowledged that coordination and accounting of these programs remains problematic.[25]

Some training, generally of individual officers, takes place in the continental United States. According to an interagency governmental working group, more than 54,000 foreign soldiers and law enforcement officials came to the United States for some form of operational training in 2000.[26] While hard data is more elusive for overseas training, it is highly probable that even more individuals are trained overseas in host countries. This includes some deployments of the US Special Operations Forces, combined military exercises or other "deployments for training" by regular US military forces, counter-drug and terrorism-related police training programs, and covert intelligence operations.

2.1 Military training in the United States

Tens of thousands of foreign military officers, as well as noncommissioned officers and cadets, come to the United States annually to study over 4,100 subjects at approximately 275 US military institutions.[27] These courses run the gamut of modern military skills—from English language training to commando skills.

In recent years, the number of countries receiving international military training from the United States has increased, as has the funding for several programs that enable countries to purchase or receive training. Some of the training is purchased from the United States by the host country, through the Department of Defense's Foreign Military Sales (FMS)[28] program or through direct commercial sales from private vendors.[29] Some of the training is provided

A sampling of international military education and training courses for selected countries

Rwanda: Command and General Staff Officer Course at the USA Command & General Staff College, Ft. Leavenworth. Curriculum includes doctrine and principles of combat, combat support, and combat service support functions. Emphasis is on war fighting at the Corps and Division level.

Turkey: Psychological Operations Course (PSYOP) at the JFK Special Warfare Center, Ft. Bragg. Curriculum includes the PSYOP process; doctrine, organization and employment; PSYOP techniques and procedures; and course exercises.

Uzbekistan: Infantry Officer Basic Course at the USA Infantry School, Ft. Benning. Curriculum includes combined arms tactics (tactical doctrine and operations, air assault operations, military operations on urban terrain); weapons (individual, special purpose, and crew served weapons); and anti-armor weapon systems.[30]

through US government grant military assistance programs, including International Military Education and Training (IMET—see section 2.1.1). The Pentagon's Foreign Military Financing grant and loan military assistance program may also be used to procure training. In addition, funding for training is sometimes provided under "emergency drawdown" authorities, which the President can use and has used frequently in recent years, in relation to counter-narcotics or peacekeeping efforts.[31]

US law requires the Departments of State, Defense and Justice to screen students in many of these programs for records of human rights violations, drug trafficking, corruption and criminal conduct. According to the Department of Defense, "US Embassy personnel, including human rights officer, regional security officer, Drug Enforcement Agency, consular section, and other offices as appropriate screen the nominees thoroughly."[32] The Security Assistance Officer that oversees the process is required to develop a checklist that encompasses the steps taken while completing background checks. This checklist is required to be kept on record for at least ten years. In addition, the Departments of State and Defense must provide Congress with annual reports on many foreign military programs, portions of which are publicly available.

Several other programs can and have been used to bring foreign military officials to the United States for military education or training, including:

- *Service academy exchanges*: One- to four-year exchange at national military academies. Up to forty foreign students may enter each of the US military academies per year.

- *Personnel Exchange Program:* One year or longer reciprocal exchange, bringing about 500 foreign military students to the United States per year.[33]

- *Unit Exchanges:* Units from foreign countries or international organizations train in the United States on a reciprocal basis (i.e., comparable US units train in the foreign country or international organization) at the direction of the military departments and combatant commands. US services conducted unit exchanges with twenty countries in 1998 and were projected to carry out exchanges with twenty-seven countries in 1999.[34] Overall numbers of personnel trained through this program are not available.

- *Subject Matter Expert Exchange Program*: Short-term exchanges of military experts, generally at the discretion of the military departments and combatant commands. Overall numbers of personnel trained through this program are not available.

- *Latin American Cooperation Program*: Two- to three-week training funded through the US military departments, intended to enhance military-to-military relationships.

In addition, the Secretary of Defense, Joint Chiefs of Staff, military departments or commanders of the Combatant Commands may designate foreign students for training in the United States as part of their responsibility to build military-to-military contacts.

Foreign students in these programs may study at any one of approximately 275 military schools and installations in the United

States, according to the Department of State. These institutions fall under all five of the military services (Army, Navy, Marine Corps, Air Force, and Coast Guard), and some fall under the purview of the Department of Defense and the Joint Chiefs of Staff. Senior service schools, colleges and academies are attended by both US and foreign senior military and civilian counterparts.

Each of the military services also has a training and doctrine command and field authority to work with its components. The US Army's Training and Doctrine Command (TRADOC), for example,

Western Hemisphere Institute for Security Cooperation at Fort Benning, Georgia (formerly US Army School of the Americas)

The Western Hemisphere Institute for Security Cooperation (WHINSEC) opened in January 2001 at the same site occupied by the US Army School of the Americas, which the Army "closed" in 2000.[35] The US Army defines the mission of WHINSEC-SOA as "provid[ing] professional education and training to eligible personnel of nations of the Western Hemisphere . . . while fostering mutual knowledge, transparency, confidence and cooperation among participating nations and promoting democratic values, respect for human rights, and knowledge and understanding of United States customs and traditions."[36]

From its inception in 1946 through January 2000, SOA graduated more than 60,000 officers, cadets and noncommissioned officers from Latin America (including some civilians). Current annual levels of attendance at WHINSEC-SOA are about 600 to 800 foreign students per year. Spanish-speaking US military officers also attend the school.[37]

The institute provides Spanish language instruction in fifty-three different courses, ranging from cadet-level instruction on intelligence to a forty-nine-week Command and General Staff Officer Course. The courses taught at WHINSEC-SOA also are taught to foreign military students at other institutions in the United States. For example, in 1995, the US Army Ranger training course was provided to forty-three foreign students from seventeen countries, exposing these students to similar training and exercises as the seventeen students who attended the School of the America's commando course.[38] In addition, six expanded IMET courses are offered at WHINSEC-SOA. (See section 3.3.3 for a more in-depth discussion of WHINSEC-SOA's courses and history.)

runs the network of twenty-seven Army schools that engage in domestic and foreign military training[39]—a network that includes WHINSEC-School of the Americas.

2.1.1 International Military Education and Training (IMET)

When asked in recent Congressional hearings which of all foreign aid programs should be allocated more funding, Secretary of State Colin Powell stated that he "would love to have more in international military education and training."[40] IMET is a security assistance program that in 2003 will grant around $80 million to more than 8,000 students from 132 countries, a 10 percent increase over 2002.[41] All foreign students in the program undergo background checks for past human rights violations.

Originally intended to build relations between US and foreign militaries and improve foreign military capabilities, IMET also has been used to teach rule of law, civil-military relations, and human rights and humanitarian law, principally through the Expanded IMET (E-IMET) program. For 2003, $1.8 million has been requested for E-IMET schools in the Western Hemisphere. Some nations, such as Guatemala and Indonesia, are eligible for E-IMET courses only.

A significant amount—perhaps up to one-quarter—of the training that takes place in the United States is on rather conventional topics, including English.[42] The majority of the training, however, relates to war-fighting skills, with a significant emphasis on military leadership courses in tactics and doctrine, logistics, and counter-insurgency techniques.

Although Congress created IMET in 1976 as a separate program in part to better measure the costs, benefits and impact of foreign military training, the US government has conducted few assessments of this program's effectiveness. In 1989, the Defense Security Assistance Agency (DSAA, since renamed the Defense Security Cooperation Agency) and the General Accounting Office (GAO) studied IMET. DSAA focused on the largely intangible benefits of the program, such as improved attitudes toward the United States. The GAO study found that there were very limited means to evaluate the effectiveness of the program and no way to determine how the training or trained personnel were used by the recipient nations.[43] A 1995

National Defense University study noted the lack of tracking or follow-up with trainees of the program.[44]

2.2 US military training abroad

While tens of thousands of individual officers receive professional or technical military training at schools in the United States, US military

Table 2
IMET funding and human rights records for select countries

Country	Funding for FY 1999	Courses offered (not inclusive)	Human rights record in 2001
Colombia	$917,000	International defense management; psychological operations; armament systems	Members of the armed forces and police continue to commit serious human rights violations; paramilitary forces still find support among the military and police.
Egypt	$1,040,000	Basic field artillery; Air War College; international defense management	Security forces committed numerous, serious human rights abuses during 2001; the government's record remains poor in several areas.
Mexico	$918,000	Basic armor officer; advanced combat army officer; armament systems	Military personnel and police officers committed mitted serious human rights abuses in 2001, including torture and killings.
Philippines	$1,348,000	Air War College; Amphibian Warfare School; psychological operations	Police and military forces committed a number of extrajudicial killings in 2001; members of the security services were responsible for disappearances and torture.
Cote d'Ivoire	$189,000	Air War College; Command & General Staff Officer; Air Command & Staff College	More than 150 extrajudicial killings were committed by security forces in 2001.[45]

forces also train alongside many tens of thousands more foreign troops abroad every year.[46]

Some of this training abroad is considered "security assistance," meant primarily and directly to benefit foreign forces. The majority, however, is considered "military-to-military contacts," meant primarily to benefit US forces or US interests. In the course of meeting these objectives, however, foreign troops receive direct operational training.

Several programs provide US training in other nations, including:

- *Counter-narcotics*: The US military provides some support and training to foreign security forces, including police, to combat drug trafficking.[47] Overall numbers of US and foreign forces involved are not made publicly available.[48] The National Defense Authorization Act for FY 2002 extended the previous year's requirement that the Secretary of Defense submit a report to Congress on all counter-drug assistance to foreign governments during the preceding year;[49] the report for FY 2001 was released March 1, 2002, and includes numbers of trainees and types of training offered.[50] The Department of Defense will submit additional reports only if Congress reauthorizes the requirement for future years.

- *Mobile training and education teams:* Mobile Training Teams (MTT) and Mobile Education Teams (MET), consisting of a small group of US military personnel, travel to countries abroad for periods of up to six months to train the host country's soldiers and officers in specific skill areas or in civil-military relations, human rights or humanitarian law. MTTs may deploy as part of weapons sales packages, training the foreign country forces in the operation and maintenance of the weapon system(s). These teams may be funded by US grants, discretionary funds from particular

> The biennial Bright Star exercise was first conducted in 1980 with US and Egyptian troops. This exercise has grown to involve more than 74,000 soldiers from ten countries.[51]

US military units or host nation funds. Background screening for MTT trainees is now required if the training is funded by US military aid programs. For privately purchased training, however, background checks are not required.

- *Deployments for training*: US military units, a portion of a unit or a composite unit can deploy to a country abroad for fifteen to forty-five days to train and work with the host nation's armed forces in some specific capability such as medical or engineering support.

- *Exercises*: US armed forces exercise extensively with foreign militaries, which the US government justifies as promoting interoperability (the ability of forces from different nations to work together in combat or other military operations). Given the large numbers of both US and foreign forces sometimes involved, screenings for human rights violations would be difficult to conduct.

- *National Guard and reserve units*: The US National Guard, a branch of the US Army in which civilians serve on a part-time basis, engages in training abroad or related exercise activities through its National Interagency Civil-Military Institute and through the National Guard State Partnership Program.[52]

- *Regional training centers and initiatives*: The US departments of the Army, Navy and Air Force, the Joint Chiefs of Staff, and the Office of the Secretary of Defense support regionally focused initiatives and centers that may train foreign military officials abroad or in the United States. Some of these initiatives, such as the African Crisis Response Initiative and the Partnership for Peace for European nations, are considered security assistance, and fund training for foreign troops in peacekeeping; coalition operations; US doctrine and defense management; counter-narcotics; and disaster response. Other programs, including the George C. Marshall European Center for Security Studies in Germany and similar centers focused on Asia-Pacific, the Western Hemisphere, Africa, and the Near East and South Asia, bring officers from various nations' militaries together to study policy. Areas of study include terrorism, weapons proliferation and professionalization of the military; there are few courses on international human rights and humanitarian law.

African Crisis Response Initiative

The African Crisis Response Initiative (ACRI) seeks to promote the ability of select African states to participate in UN or regional peacekeeping operations by providing battalion- and brigade-level training and equipment.[53] Participating militaries undergo an initial sixty- to seventy-day training phase and up to five follow-up trainings. US Special Operations Forces from the 3rd or 5th Special Forces groups have conducted basic training for, and evaluation of, the armed forces of all ACRI nations except Ethiopia, which was suspended from the program because of its war with Eritrea. As of mid-2001, US forces (in conjunction with some private contractors) had trained over 800 soldiers in Senegal, Uganda (suspended in 1998 from further training because of the presence of Ugandan forces in the Democratic Republic of the Congo), Benin, Cote d'Ivoire (suspended in 1999 because of a military coup), Ghana, Kenya, Malawi, and Mali. After receiving criticism from some Members of Congress and US government officials that ACRI was too limited, the State Department introduced for FY 2003 a request for $10 million to initiate a comprehensive US crisis response training program to succeed ACRI. In addition to teaching peacekeeping and humanitarian operations, the new program would provide the basis for lethal peace enforcement training. Potential recipients include, but are not limited to, Botswana, Ghana, Kenya, Senegal, and Tanzania.[54]

2.2.1 Special Operations Forces and Joint Combined Exchange Training (JCET)

In recent years, overseas deployment of US Special Operations Forces (SOF) have grown dramatically, including deployments for training of foreign militaries. In FY 1991, SOF deployed to 92 countries; eight years later (FY 1999), they trained in 152 countries— not including classified missions.[55] Between 1991 and 1997, as other parts of the military services were cut, SOF grew by 10,000 soldiers, and its budget grew by $1 billion (from $2.4 billion to $3.4 billion).[56]

Today, in an average week, between 2,000 and 3,000 SOF personnel are deployed on 150 missions in 60 to 70 countries.[57]

Special Operations Forces, which include the Navy Sea-Air Land Teams (SEALs), Army Rangers, Army Special Forces (Green Berets) and other units, differ from other military forces in that they are organized, trained and equipped to achieve certain kinds of missions, sometimes described as "unconventional warfare,"[58] a range of activities including sabotage, hostage rescue, covert reconnaissance for locating military targets, landmine removal, and humanitarian relief. A number of SOF missions include direct cooperation and interaction with foreign forces, including using foreign forces as surrogates for military or combat missions, building positive views of the United States through civil affairs and "psychological operations," and assisting other nations with Foreign Internal Defense or suppressing "subversion, lawlessness and insurgency."[59]

Although much SOF activity remains classified, publicly available information indicates that US SOF have continued to train with military forces known to have recently committed serious human rights violations in the context of armed conflict—in Colombia, Indonesia, Sri Lanka, Turkey and elsewhere.

One of the key SOF foreign training programs is Joint Combined Exchange Training (JCET), which was designed to allow SOF to practice foreign language skills, to gain familiarity with foreign militaries and terrain, and to train foreign personnel.[60] Authorized by the US Congress in 1991, the program permits regional Combatant Commanders and the Commander of the Special Operations Command to fund deployment and training of SOF abroad, including the participation of foreign troops, as long as the primary purpose of the activity is to train US forces.[61] This requirement is the only limiting condition on JCETs.

In JCET deployments, US SOF teams—from six to thirty soldiers, generally—train with host nation units for two weeks to a month, and sometimes longer. In FY 1999, SOF conducted 124 JCETs, training 17,000 foreign personnel. The budget for this activity is $12 million to $15 million annually.[62]

The law authorizing the JCET program requires an annual report to Congress. Even with this reporting requirement, public knowledge and official oversight of the program was minimal until a 1998 series of articles in *The Washington Post* publicized that SOF were training foreign troops in countries that Congress had barred from the International Military Education and Training program.[63] Subsequent Congressional criticism has centered on claims that the program undermines human rights and democratization programs of the United States and host governments, and specifically that it circumvented Congressional intent regarding a ban, on human rights grounds, on training Indonesian forces.[64] At a 1998 hearing in the US House of Representatives, for example, Representative Chris Smith of New Jersey labeled the SOF training of Indonesian forces "unbelievably baffling and dismaying," in light of the human rights violations attributed to the same forces by the State Department in its annual Country Reports on human rights practices. Smith noted that such training indicated that political reform and human rights protection were not the Administration's highest priority.[65] Revelations about US SOF training of Rwandan troops later implicated in mass killings in eastern Zaire[66] also raised Congressional concern.

In 1998, the US Congress enacted legislation that required the Secretary of Defense to give prior approval to any JCET and excluded from training any foreign security force unit credibly implicated in human rights abuses. These laws are reportedly actively implemented within the Departments of State and Defense,[67] although there is no human rights requirement for other types of SOF training of foreign forces.

2.3 Police training

From 1962 to 1974, the Office of Public Safety at the Agency for International Development provided training for over one million police personnel from thirty-four countries in criminal investigation, patrolling, interrogation and counter-insurgency techniques, riot control, and weapon use.[68] During its thirteen years of operation, the program sent approximately $325 million in training and equipment overseas.[69]

In 1973, Congress prohibited the use of foreign assistance funds for police training in all foreign countries in the face of mounting evidence that training and equipment provided under the Public Safety program were directly supporting governments implicated in widespread human rights abuses, particularly in Latin America. This provision did not apply, however, to the Departments of Justice, Transportation, and Treasury, including the Federal Bureau of Investigation and the Drug Enforcement Agency, all of which are authorized and funded from budgets other than foreign assistance. Additionally, a number of exceptions were made to the 1973 law over time, such as US police training in Haiti under the government of Jean-Claude Duvalier. By 1990, the US General Accounting Office was able to identify 125 countries that received police training financed by US taxpayers, despite the legislative "ban."[70]

Today, several agencies train tens of thousands of foreign police and law enforcement officials for a variety of reasons. All police trainees, like military trainees funded via the annual foreign assistance or Department of Defense budgets passed by Congress,[71]

Table 3[72]
Police forces cited in the State Department's country reports on human rights

Country	Funding for International Narcotics Control and Law Enforcement in 2000[73]	Human rights violations committed by police forces in 2001
Laos	$4,000,000	Arbitrary arrest and detention, incommunicado detention, torture and other abuse.
Thailand	$3,000,000	Beating, use of excessive force, involvement in prostitution and trafficking in women and children.
Colombia	$894,429,000	Extrajudicial killings, collusion with paramilitary forces, social cleansing murders.
Brazil	$5,000,000	Extrajudicial killings, torture and beating of suspects, killings for hire, death squad executions, narcotics trafficking.
Bolivia	$158,000,000	Torture, use of excessive force, arbitrary arrest and detention, killings during demonstrations.
Pakistan	$3,250,000	Extrajudicial killings, abuse, rape, torture, arbitrary arrest and detention.

go through background checks to ensure that the program is not training police or soldiers with records of past human rights abuses. Police training programs, which are conducted both in the United States and in other countries, include

- *International Narcotics Control and Law Enforcement:* For FY 2003, the Department of seeks $928 million from Congress under the broad heading of "International Narcotics Control and Law Enforcement." Although the Department of State manages the program, the Drug Enforcement Administration (DEA), the US Customs Service and the US Coast Guard conduct the actual training. Since 1971, the Bureau of International Narcotics and Law Enforcement in the Department of State has transferred over $120 million to these agencies for the training of more than 70,000 foreign officials.[74] In FY 2002, recipients of this training included forces from Bolivia, Colombia, Ecuador, Hungary, Laos, Pakistan, Peru, Thailand, Turkey, Venezuela, Vietnam, several countries in East Asia and a number of nations in Africa.[75]

- *Antiterrorism Assistance:* The State Department's request for this program for FY 2003 is $64.2 million, a marked increase from FY 2002.[76] The program provides weapons, equipment and training to foreign law enforcement operations in Egypt, Israel, Jordan, Kenya, Kyrgyzstan, the Persian Gulf states, Tanzania, Uganda, and Uzbekistan, among others.[77] The Department of State reported in February 2002 that, in all, more than 28,000 foreign law enforcement personnel have received training through this program.[78] The Department of State is also seeking to establish a Center for Antiterrorism and Security Training (CAST), which would enable it to expand this type of training.

- *International Crime:* The Federal Bureau of Investigation's International Training Section administers international mission-oriented training in coordination with other FBI operational divisions, the Office of International Programs in the Department of Justice, the Department of State, and overseas US embassies. These international training initiatives include country evaluations and/or needs analyses and training of foreign law enforcement officials both within the United States and abroad. Two specific international training programs that the FBI carries out are the Pacific Rim Training Initiative and the Mexican/American Law Enforcement Training Initiative.[79] The latter involves training the 5,000-member Mexican Federal Preventive Police, a unit that media accounts have implicated in human rights abuses, including torture, in Guerrero state.[80] Because it is not funded from the

Police training in Northern Ireland

Patrick Finucane was shot dead by the paramilitary Ulster Freedom Fighters in 1989. Rosemary Nelson was killed by a car bomb in March 1999 in the town of Lurgan, Northern Ireland. Although ten years separated their murders, evidence has emerged in recent years that the killings of both of these human rights lawyers took place with collusion by the police (Royal Ulster Constabulary) and the UK army. In addition to the United Nations and several other international bodies, the US Congress has called on the United Kingdom government to establish independent judicial inquiries into their deaths.[81] In 1999, as part of the foreign aid budget appropriation for the year 2000, Congress barred the FBI and any other federal law enforcement agency from using any federal funds to provide any training (including exchange programs) for the Royal Ulster Constabulary (RUC), or any successor organization to the RUC. The ban was motivated by concerns that the FBI may have trained forces that committed or condoned the murders of Rosemary Nelson and Patrick Finucane, or otherwise perpetrated or seriously threatened violence against defense attorneys in Northern Ireland. The law required the President to submit a detailed report on all training or exchange programs conducted for the RUC or RUC members from 1994 to 1999. Training may be resumed in the future to the reconfigured North Ireland forces only if such programs include a significant human rights component and include vetting procedures to ensure that training or exchange programs do not include RUC members if there are substantial grounds for believing they might have committed or condoned violations of internationally recognized human rights.[82]

foreign assistance or Department of Defense budgets, FBI training appears to be exempt from human rights screening.

2.3.1 International Criminal Investigative Training Assistance Program (ICITAP)

Originally designed to improve law enforcement agencies in Latin America and the Caribbean, the International Criminal Investigative Training Assistance Program launched its first major program in Panama in 1989, following the US capture of then-President Manuel Noriega. Its training programs now span the globe.

Based in the Criminal Division of the Department of Justice, ICITAP programs are developed by the Departments of Justice and State and funded from the annual foreign aid budget. The National Security Council, as well as the Departments of State and Justice, approves ICITAP projects, at the request of or with the consent of the host government.

There are two principle types of projects. ICITAP projects in the Balkans, Haiti, and Panama, for example, are aimed at achieving a wholesale transformation of a law enforcement's institutional culture by shifting the agency focus from "service to the state" to "democratic principles of policing as a service and protection of the people." Other ICITAP projects, such as those in Bolivia, Colombia, South Africa and the former Soviet states, are aimed at providing specific technical assistance.[83]

In 1999, ICITAP trained 8,000 foreign law enforcement officials, with a budget of $35 million. The program continued a major police reform project in Haiti, and its single biggest project seeks to create an effective civil police force, trained in international humanitarian and human rights law and standards, in Kosovo.[84] ICITAP projects are funded from various parts of the annual foreign aid budget, and participants are subject to background reviews for past human rights violations.

2.4 Intelligence agencies training police and military forces

In the National Security Act of 1947, Congress provided authority for the Executive Branch of the US government to engage in covert or semi-covert military operations.[85] Historically, the Central Intelligence Agency has advised, trained, and equipped government forces implicated in large-scale human rights abuses in many countries, including the military of the Republic of Vietnam during the Vietnam War; the Iranian secret police (SAVAK) under Shah Reza Pahlavi; the Chilean secret police under General Augusto Pinochet (DINA); and the Nicaraguan National Guard under president Anastasio Somoza.[86]

The CIA also sent training, agents, and materials to support armed opposition groups in Albania, Guatemala, Laos, Poland, Soviet Ukraine, as well as indirectly to Afghanistan (via Pakistan), Angola (via Zaire), and Nicaragua (via El Salvador, Guatemala, and Honduras). In each of the last three cases, recipients of CIA training and weapons have been implicated in widespread violations of humanitarian law, including extrajudicial killings, torture, disappearances, and other gross violations of human rights.[87]

According to the 1996 report of the official US Commission on Roles and Capabilities of the United States Intelligence Community, "Since the end of the Cold War, the number and size of covert action programs have shrunk substantially. . . . Nonetheless, these programs continue to be undertaken to support ongoing policy needs."[88] In recent years, the media has reported on covert CIA involvement in training operations in the "front line states" surrounding Sudan, with the Kosovo Liberation Army in Albania prior to the NATO bombing,[89] and in Iraqi Kurdistan.[90] The intelligence community is also involved in training foreign forces involved in counter-narcotics operations.

Ideas and plans for most covert operations are developed by a special staff within the Central Intelligence Agency's Directorate of Operations (DO). Before such an action can be initiated, the President must make a "finding" that the operation is vital to US national security.

In most cases the CIA is also responsible for implementation, but various military services and other agencies within the intelligence community have carried out covert actions as well. According to a 1997 report on intelligence community reform, the DO has maintained "highly collaborative" relations with all branches of the armed forces, particularly the Army Special Forces.[91] The CIA also has developed and managed its own paramilitary capabilities, largely through the use of private companies and soldiers for hire.[92]

The National Security Act requires very little Congressional oversight of covert intelligence agency operations. Section 505 of the Act simply requires the Central Intelligence Agency, or other government agencies engaging in such activities, to notify in a "timely fashion" the Congressional committees responsible for oversight of US intelligence community activities of any arms supply operation (including training) undertaken valued at $1 million or more.

There is no official public reporting on covert intelligence community military and police training operations and no public accountability. In the past, many of these operations have been exposed through the media, court documents, foreign governmental records and—eventually—through declassification of US government documents.[93] The Human Rights Information Act, a bill first proposed during the 106th Congress in 1999, would order the expedited declassification of human rights information related to US intelligence activities in Honduras and Guatemala, and establish a process for future human rights information requests in other countries.[94]

2.5 Private commercial contractors training military and police

The US government also hires or authorizes private military consultants to train foreign police forces and military troops. According to one source, US companies trained military forces in more than 24 countries during the 1990s, including Angola, Bolivia, Bosnia, Colombia, Croatia, Egypt, Equatorial Guinea, Ethiopia, Haiti, Kosovo, Liberia, Nigeria, Peru, Rwanda, and Saudi Arabia—nations with histories of human rights violations by military and police forces.

In many cases, the US Departments of Defense, Justice and State hire private corporations to implement government-designed training projects. For example, the Department of State works with Military Professional Resources International (MPRI) and Logicon to train countries involved in its African Crisis Response Initiative (ACRI). Similarly, many training missions related to the US-funded war on drugs are being contracted privately.[95]

In addition to working for the US government to carry out training programs, private companies may also contract directly with foreign governments to train military, security, or police forces independent of the US government. To do so, firms must first apply for and be granted an export license by the State Department's Office of Defense Trade Controls.[96] Companies ranging from Boeing to MPRI apply for training contracts—Boeing for training on weapons systems it manufactures, and MPRI for training in tactics and operations.

A sampling of private US Companies involved in military training outside the US[97]

BDM: Acquired in 1997 by TRW, a defense industry giant with 94,000 employees and about $16 billion in annual revenue. Philip Odeen, former CEO and president of BDM and also a veteran of the National Security Council and Department of Defense, now holds a position in TRW management. TRW has also acquired the Vinnell Corporation, another military training provider.

Booz-Allen & Hamilton: Established in 1914, with over 10,000 employees and $2 billion in annual revenue.

Carlyle Group: Established in 1987, a global investment firm capitalized at more than $12.5 billion. Managing Director and Chairman Frank C. Carlucci is a former National Security Advisor and former Secretary of Defense.

DFI International: Established in 1984 as a consulting firm and listing "foreign military assessments" among its services. Former Department of Defense Comptroller William Lynn recently joined its management team as a vice president.

DynCorp: Established in 1946 with more than $1.8 billion in annual revenues and 23,000 employees. Among the largest employee-owned technology and services companies in the United States.

Military Professional Resources International: Established in 1989, currently with 800 employees. The majority of senior management has military or law enforcement experience, including President Carl E. Vuono, former Chief of Staff of the US Army.

Science Applications International Corporation: Established in 1969, with more than $5 billion in annual revenues and 40,000 employees.

Texas Instruments: Employs more than 35,400 people, with total annual revenues of about $3 billion.

In 1975 Vinnell Corporation became the first private American company to receive permission from the State Department to run an independent training program for a foreign security force—in this case the Saudi Arabian National Guard.[98] Vinnell's most recent contract with Saudi Arabia is for 1998-2003, and the firm currently has around 1,400 civilian employees in that country.[99] Several other foreign militaries and police forces have hired private US companies for training. According to a newspaper report in early 2000, DynCorp Inc. and MPRI were then completing contracts for logistical support and training of Colombian police and counter-insurgency forces, while at least six US firms had set up operations in Latin America, in anticipation of lucrative new contracts related to the United States' $1.6 billion military aid program for Colombia.[100]

The level of public transparency and accountability is significantly higher for US government programs that employ private contractors, such as the ACRI program, than it is for private commercial transactions between foreign entities and private US firms. Information on private transactions is scarce. There is no requirement that the US Department of State publish an annual listing of precisely whom it has licensed (and therefore authorized) to provide private military or security training, for what purpose, where and with which security unit. The US Congress is not informed of who is training whom, since the State Department is only required to notify lawmakers of contracts valued at $50 million or more—a threshold so high that very few, if any, training operations are likely to surpass it.

Moreover, commercial training contracts are exempt from disclosure under the Freedom of Information Act, the law that allows the US public to petition the US government for the release of documents. Military companies can block and have blocked public access to information on commercially negotiated contracts by arguing that even the most basic information is proprietary.

In some cases, a local US Embassy's security assistance office may make a field visit to observe a private military contractor's training program. Oversight is at the discretion of each embassy, however, and varies greatly.

Private military training in Croatia

In 1995, Croatian soldiers involved in military operations in the Krajina area of Croatia committed a number of serious human rights violations against the local Croatian Serb population, including killing, torturing, and raping civilians.[101] These violations occurred in the context of surprisingly successful military operations, called "Flash" and "Storm," in which the Croatian military had exhibited new communications techniques and troop movements that did not resemble its usual Warsaw Pact military tactics.[102]

The year before, an American consultant, Military Professional Resources International (MPRI), had received a two-year contract from Croatia (later extended for two more years) for the "Democracy Transition Assistance Program" (DTAP). This privately contracted program between MPRI and the Croatian government was supposed to ensure that the Croatian military could meet the necessary human rights and democracy standards for admission into NATO's "Partnership for Peace" program. DTAP was to focus on classroom teaching of issues such as the difference between military and civil systems of law and proper military conduct toward civilians during and after conflict. No classes on tactics or on the use of weaponry were to be taught.

In May 1996 Amnesty International USA sent a letter to the head of MPRI and to the US Secretary of State, raising several questions about the human rights situation in Croatia (and in Bosnia, where MPRI was also training forces) and inquiring about MPRI's human rights training. "The fact that MPRI's initial training was followed by human rights violations [in Croatia], raises serious questions about the effectiveness of the human rights component of the training offered by MPRI," the letter said. It asked specifically about the firm's system of vetting trainees, the content of the training (in particular inquiring whether the training raised the issue of gender, given widespread rape committed during the war in the region), and how the impact and effectiveness of the training were monitored.[103]

AIUSA staff subsequently met with MPRI International Vice President Ed Soyster, who said that there was no specific human rights training included in the training provided to the Croatian forces. He also made the point that as a private organization, MPRI was not accountable to Amnesty International or to anyone else for the content of its training programs.

The following year Amnesty International USA filed a series of requests for information from the US State Department's Office of the Special Representative for Military Stabilization in the Balkans, asking about the human rights components of the MPRI's Croatia contracts. AIUSA received no substantive information from the Special Representative's office.[104]

There are no legal or regulatory requirements for the inclusion of any human rights or humanitarian law content in military, security, or police force training contracted privately. In addition, Congressionally-mandated requirements that trainees be vetted for prior human rights abuses do not apply to privately funded and contracted training. These requirements do apply, however, to US taxpayer-funded programs employing private firms, such as ACRI.

3
Human rights training and the US government

"I was not surprised, in September 1999, when I read in an Associated Press article that American troops had killed South Korean civilians at a hamlet called No Gun Ri in the chaotic early days of the Korean War. When the dogs of war are let loose, civilians always suffer. . . . What did surprise me was the allegation that the killings appeared to be deliberate; I found it difficult to believe that American soldiers would kill unarmed refugees. In the months that followed, however, as one of eight outside observers asked to monitor a Pentagon investigation of the issue, I came full circle. The investigation confirmed the news report's central charges."

—Lt. Gen. Bernard E. Trainor (USMC, ret.),
The Washington Post, January 21, 2001

In January 2001, the US Army Inspector General released a report on No Gun Ri, a Korean hamlet where in 1950, American soldiers allegedly massacred unarmed refugees during the Korean War. The Army's report concluded that the "under-trained, under-equipped and unprepared" US soldiers had, in fact, fired on Korean civilians. According to the Army, the American soldiers at No Gun Ri were "completely unprepared for the stark reality of dealing with the numerous, uncontrolled refugees who clogged the roads and complicated the battlefield to an unexpected degree."[105]

No Gun Ri illustrates the danger of leaving to chance the ability of a military force to interact with civilians during the stress and confusion of combat. The killings at No Gun Ri occurred over 50 years ago, but the underlying dangers that led to those killings are still very much current. Until recently, however, the US government had few requirements or practices for including human rights content in training provided to foreign security and police forces. This chapter examines the growing network of human rights law that governs US training of foreign militaries, current human rights content in education and training, and human rights considerations in operational training. The final section of the chapter offers three case studies of recent or ongoing US training relationships with forces that have been directly implicated in gross violations of human rights.

3.1 The legal framework and the Leahy Law

A network of laws governs US military assistance and sales to foreign countries, including the Arms Export Control Act and the Foreign Assistance Act. The Arms Export Control Act of 1976 stipulates that arms transfers should "strengthen the security of the United States and promote world peace." The Act further notes that weapons may be transferred to countries only for purposes of "legitimate" self-defense, internal security, internal civil works, and collective security arrangements or UN operations. The Foreign Assistance Act of 1961 outlines the provisions of all economic and military assistance to foreign governments, including specific language barring aid or arms sales to any country that shows "gross and consistent violations of internationally recognized human rights."

In addition to this overall legal framework, an amendment to annual Foreign Operations and Defense Appropriations Acts, also known as the "Leahy Law," specifically prohibits the transfer of US aid to foreign security, military, and police units where there is credible evidence linking such units to human rights violations.

The "Leahy Law," named for its original sponsor, US Senator Patrick Leahy of Vermont, was first introduced in 1996 following the public release of documents proving that the United States had given aid to Colombian army units implicated in human rights violations, despite Clinton Administration assurances to the contrary in 1994.[106] The original iteration of the Leahy Law required that all recipients of US training and equipment through the International Narcotics Control program were to be vetted, or screened, for credible allegations of past human rights abuses. This requirement was expanded in 1998 to all forms of security assistance funded out of the foreign affairs budget. In 1999 the law was extended to counter-narcotics and some other military training provided through the

Defense Department budget, including, for example, JCET [Joint Combined Exchange Training (see section 2.2.1)] operations.[107]

Today, both the US Departments of State and Defense have procedures in place to comply with the Leahy Law. For a JCET, for example, the commanders-in-chief of the regional commands request the US Embassy in the country where a JCET activity is to take place to gather and evaluate credible information on the human rights record of the unit to be trained. The regional commander then submits to the Secretary of Defense the following statement: "The Embassy certifies that the Department of State possesses no credible information of gross violations of human rights by the (name of designated unit), or a member of that unit, as of this date."[108] The Secretary of Defense is then required by law to review the information and approve each JCET.

In December 1997 the Departments of State and Defense also established a vetting procedure for IMET [International Military Education and Training (see section 2.1.1)] students after the US Congress included this requirement in the 1998 Foreign Operations Appropriations Act (Public Law 105-118). The two departments transmitted a joint cable to all US embassies that outlined specific guidelines regarding screening of prospective students attending US-sponsored military training—including training at the then School of the Americas. These guidelines require that the:

- host nation government checks the background of any student it nominates to attend an IMET program;
- US country team (US defense attaché and other Embassy officials) checks the nominated student's background;
- US country team interviews the nominated student; and
- US country team maintains records of the screening checklist for ten years.

These requirements apply to all countries receiving any training financed through the United States' annual foreign aid and defense budgets (including IMET and Foreign Military Financing, most forms of police training, counter-terrorism training, peacekeeping training, counter-narcotics training and personnel exchange programs).[109] However, for non-US-funded military trainees in the United States— apparently the vast majority of international military students here—there is still no vetting procedure.

In practice, procedures for conducting background checks vary from embassy to embassy.[110] In general, host governments nominate the students to be trained, although the embassy is required to approve the selection in consultation with the US defense attaché.[111] The process for deciding which courses they will take varies, but the security assistance officer in the embassy is encouraged to maintain an active dialogue with the host country in order to develop a training plan that takes into account both the host country's objectives and specific US program objectives. The Defense Security Cooperation Agency and other Department of Defense offices also provide guidance in program planning.[112]

The quality of the background vetting depends on the interest and the commitment of the Ambassador, the level of effort of embassy staff, and the availability of full and reliable information about prospective students. Although not required to do so, some US embassy staff will contact national or international human rights organizations in reviewing potential military students' backgrounds.

Many of the skills and knowledge foreign students learn in US courses are transferable. In fact, the US military often employs a "train the trainer" strategy, whereby training recipients are expected to share their learned skills with other troops in their home military, police or security force. This type of training currently is being proposed as part of US training for the new Afghan army.[113] The impact of such training on home units is difficult to verify, particularly since the US government does not systematically track the careers and contributions of alumni of its training programs.

Given the uneven application of standards for assessing eligibility for training, the overall human rights situation in nations receiving training should be taken into account.[114] For example, "re-transfer" of US training would be of particular concern in cases of states engaged in armed conflict with a history of human rights abuses. Afghanistan, with its recent history of internal armed conflicts among various factions, provides an example of potential dangers.

3.2 Follow-up tracking of past trainees

The US government has conducted limited assessment of the impact of its training programs on individual foreign soldiers and military units trained. This situation continues, although nations participating in IMET training agree that trainees will be utilized in the national military education and training system of the recipient nation for at least two years upon their return home. The lack of follow-up also means that the US government historically has been unable to measure the success of its own programs and demonstrate the claimed benefits of a training relationship, and of IMET in particular.

From a human rights perspective, tracking major career developments of foreign military trainees is essential for understanding the relationship between US training and human rights abuses or other criminal activity. Such data may not show a causal relationship, because many different factors generally contribute to an individual's or government's decision to take action that violates international law and human rights standards. But such data would provide a measure of accountability for US programs for the benefit of both the US government and US public. This tracking can help the US government assess the effectiveness of its courses, programs, trainers, and venues in promoting and protecting human rights and other stated goals.

Legislation enacted in October 2000 required the Secretary of Defense to begin tracking all foreign military or defense ministry civilian personnel who receive IMET education and training as of January 1, 2001. Also as of January 2001, the Department of Defense began developing a database of records on each IMET trainee, including the type of instruction received, the dates of instruction and "to the extent practicable, a record of the person's subsequent military or defense ministry career and current position and location."[115] This information is not publicly accessible,[116] and there is currently no requirement to report the information to Congress.

None of the other training and exchange programs discussed in this report require any US government assessment. For cash-paying military

trainees in the United States, there are currently no end-use requirements for US training, no follow-up on trainees, and no records
of trainees. For JCET exercises, which train small units rather than
individuals, Pentagon officials have made conflicting claims about
tracking trainees.[117] A nongovernmental organization, the School of
the Americas Watch Campaign, has demonstrated that such tracking
is possible, even with limited resources (see section 3.3.3).

3.3 Human rights content in education and training

There is no systematic requirement for any human rights content
in the majority of US military training and education provided to
foreign forces. Indeed, since most training of foreign security forces
is purchased, there may be no human rights content at all in most
US training of foreign nationals. The two exceptions to this general
rule are IMET and the WHINSEC-School of the Americas.

Before examining the human rights training provided to foreign
military forces, it is helpful to understand how American forces are
trained in human rights, humanitarian law and civil-military
relations. As a state party to the Geneva Conventions of 1949 (on
protections afforded to non-combatants and to prisoners of war)
and to the 1907 Hague Convention Respecting the Laws and Customs
of War on Land, the United States is obligated to train its military
forces to respect the laws of war.

In accordance with this obligation, US forces began receiving
some training in the international humanitarian law of war in the
1950s.[118] The Peers Commission, which investigated the 1968 My Lai
Massacre in Vietnam, found that the principles of law had not been
incorporated into all levels of operational training.

In 1974, the Department of Defense issued a directive requiring
all US military personnel to receive training in the laws of war
commensurate with their duties and responsibilities (described by
one US military officer as "a stair step approach," with more
advanced officers receiving more such training).[119] According to an
early 1990s assessment by the Washington Office on Latin America,
"There is widespread agreement that training was consequently
systematized, expanded and taken more seriously in all the armed
services. Training in the laws of war is now institutionalized in

all Army schools, with follow up in annual reviews, and training exercises have been modified to convey laws of war requirements, such as introducing civilians into battlefield scenarios."[120]

Recent controversies over the conduct of US forces in Iraq in 1990 and 1991[121] and Pentagon handling of revelations at No Gun Ri[122] raise the possibility, however, that human rights and humanitarian principles may not be incorporated into operational training as fully as US government officials and the general public believed. Furthermore, the failure of the US Army to hold anyone

The My Lai massacre

On March 16, 1968, US soldiers entered the Vietnamese village of My Lai in an apparent attempt to find and destroy the Viet Cong's 48th Battalion, but instead killed approximately 500 of the village's 700 residents. Among the victims were older women praying at a temple and children who were shot at point-blank range. Many others were executed en masse. When Chief Warrant Officer Hugh Thompson arrived at the village and witnessed the numerous dead and dying civilians, he immediately reported to brigade headquarters. In the meantime, the killings continued, with Lieutenant William Calley giving orders to other soldiers to kill 70 to 80 men, women and children who had been brought to a drainage ditch at the eastern edge of the village. Thompson told his helicopter crew chief to "open up on the Americans" if they fired at the civilians, and then succeeded in rescuing ten Vietnamese, including five children and an infant. After an attempted cover-up of the killings, the Pentagon began a closed-door investigation headed by General William Peers. Months of interviewing witnesses preceded release of the Peers Report, which criticized the actions of both officers and enlisted men. The report recommended action against dozens of men for rape, murder, or participation in the cover-up. Calley was found guilty of premeditated murder and sentenced to life in prison, but he was released on parole in 1974.[123] In addition, the Peers Report concluded that many soldiers in the 11th Brigade were not adequately trained in:

a) Their responsibilities regarding obedience to orders of their superiors that they considered palpably illegal;

b) Their responsibilities concerning the procedures for reporting war crimes;

c) The provisions of the Geneva Conventions, the handling and treatment of prisoners of war, and the treatment and safeguarding of noncombatants.[124]

accountable for the preparation, dissemination and use of training manuals advocating torture and other human rights violations (see section 3.3.3) sends a signal to other militaries that impunity for violations is acceptable. It may also communicate that violations are only a problem when they receive public attention.

In December 1998 the Deputy Secretary of Defense issued a directive on the Department of Defense's "Law of War Program," which updates the United States' compliance with its obligations under the Geneva Conventions and other laws of warfare. According to the directive, all possible, suspected, or alleged violations of the laws of war committed by or against US or enemy personnel are to be promptly reported, thoroughly investigated and remedied by corrective action. All alleged violations by or against persons in a conflict where US personnel are present but not a party—for example, present in a training or advisory capacity—are to be reported through command channels and expeditiously conveyed to appropriate US agencies, allied governments or "other appropriate authorities." The directive states that "on scene commanders shall ensure that measures are taken to preserve evidence of reportable incidents pending turnover to US, allied or other appropriate authorities."[125] The Secretary of the Army is responsible for collecting all reports and investigations of alleged incidents violating the laws of war.

This directive also holds "heads of Department of Defense components" responsible for ensuring that subordinates "comply with the law of war during all armed conflicts, however such conflicts are characterized, and with the principles and spirit of the law of war during all other operations."[126]

There is no requirement, however, that the substance and spirit of this directive be applied to the training of foreign nationals. The Department of Defense does not require that foreign military students attending US schools demonstrate a basic understanding of international humanitarian law and internationally accepted norms of human rights.

3.3.1 International Military Education and Training (IMET)

IMET is one of the few programs that does incorporate human rights content into training offered to foreign students. In 1978 Congress added human rights promotion to the list of objectives for IMET, making it the only training program at that time with such a goal.

The cornerstone of the IMET human rights training is informal exposure to US culture, values and civil-military operations through a DoD-managed Informational Program (IP)[127]—what one critic has called the "osmosis" theory of human rights training.[128]

Under this decentralized system, International Military Student Officers (IMSOs) at each of the 275 installations involved in military training implement locally focused programs designed to appeal to foreign military students. Examples from the Informational Program at a US army ammunition school in Illinois during the mid-1990s included:

- a speech by Elie Wiesel;
- an event commemorating Martin Luther King Day;
- attendance at a political debate;
- a tour of a county jail;
- a tour of a state capital;
- a tour of a newspaper company; and
- a trip to a local farm to discuss land use and ownership issues.

Informational Program activities are guided by a 1994 handbook that suggests teaching material and offers lessons learned from previous interactions with foreign students. In practice, Informational Programs vary tremendously from training institution to training institution, and from IMSO to IMSO. According to a 1993 study, a list of IP-approved activities in the early 1990s at the School of the Americas, for example, included sporting events, a visit to Six Flags amusement park and a tour of a local arms manufacturing plant.[129]

The Informational Program is not included in a school's formal training schedule as either a block of instruction or an elective, but rather is normally fitted around the existing curriculum. Participation in the program is apparently voluntary,[130] and a memo sent to all Army school commandants in 1995 placed secondary emphasis on the Informational Program.[131]

In a 1990 report, the General Accounting Office (GAO) of the US Congress found that approximately half of the foreign military students it questioned regarding human rights training did not recall receiving *any* human rights education while attending military training courses in the United States. The GAO recommended adding to the Informational Program a mechanism to evaluate the effectiveness of the human rights awareness training included in IMET and development of programs that provide more specific human rights education available to international students.[132] This recommendation has not been implemented by the US Congress or the Department of Defense by May 2002.

3.3.2 Expanded IMET

By 1990, Members of Congress had become increasingly concerned that US military training of foreign personnel could erode military respect for civilian authority in trainees' home countries.[133] As a result, Congress enacted legislation to limit traditional "internal defense" training, and to emphasize training in the skills and concepts required for countries to become successful democracies. These included:

- civil-military relations (the military's role in a democratic society);
- human rights;
- defense resource management;
- military justice; and
- education of civilians to oversee and work with the military.

The Foreign Operations Appropriations Act for FY 1991 mandated that not less than $1 million of IMET funds be set aside for:

> developing, initiating, conducting, and evaluating courses and other programs for training foreign civilian and military officials in managing and administering foreign military establishments and budgets, and for training foreign military and civilian officials in creating and maintaining effective military judicial systems and military codes of conduct, including observance of internationally recognized human rights . . . [Civilian personnel] shall include foreign government personnel of ministries other than ministries of defense if the military education and training would (i) contribute to responsible defense resource management, (ii) foster greater respect for and understanding of the principle of civilian control of the military, or (iii) improve military justice systems and procedures in accordance with internationally recognized human rights.

According to Department of Defense testimony in 1999, expanded IMET (E-IMET) has grown to 30 percent of the IMET budget, which would place spending on E-IMET in FY 2003 at an estimated $24 million.

The Defense Security Cooperation Agency (DSCA) is responsible for the development and certification of courses for the expanded IMET program. Security assistance officers (or military groups) in host nations are responsible for the promotion of foreign military and civilian attendance. A certain percentage of all countries' IMET program must be selected from the approved expanded IMET courses. This percentage varies by country and is subject to approval by the DSCA.[134] For a country whose international military training program is extremely politically sensitive, the entire IMET program may consist of E-IMET training, as is currently the case with Indonesia[135] and Guatemala.

Thirty-three institutions across the United States offer courses that qualify as E-IMET. Among these are the Western Hemisphere Institute for Security Cooperation-SOA, which offers six E-IMET courses, and the JFK Special Warfare School at Ft. Bragg, which offers one course, called "Civil Affairs." However, the majority of E-IMET courses are offered at three schools:

- *Defense Resource Management Institute (DRMI)*, located at the Naval Postgraduate School in Monterey, California, was charged with meeting the E-IMET need to help recipient countries establish processes for more effective defense resource management. DRMI established a Mobile Education Team (MET), which is responsible for presenting course curricula in countries and developing resident programs within the United States, including an eleven-week, mid-level course and a four-week senior course, open to high- ranking military officers and civilian counterparts.

- *The Naval Justice School,* under the direction of the Department of Defense, has established a program to address military justice and human rights topics. A multi-phased program comprised of traveling seminars and resident programs was designed to culminate in the passage of amended military codes by national legislatures in participating students' home countries. In October 1995, Albania became the first nation to enact a rewritten military code under this program. The Naval Justice School conducted this program in at least 50 countries during FY 1997.

- *The Center for Civil-Military Relations (CCMR)* is also located at the Naval Postgraduate School in Monterey, California. It was established by the DSCA to provide a broad range of graduate-level educational programs and research that address specific issues of civil-military relations in a democratic society. Initially, this program is conducted as a one-week seminar held in the host nation. Ministers, key parliamentarians, ranking military representatives, and the US Ambassador attend the program. It is followed by resident programs in the United States, including an accelerated one-year graduate degree program. The program's first class was held in January 1996.

E-IMET is often taught through Mobile Education Teams visiting host countries for two weeks. According to one assessment, these local trainings often bring together civil society and the military for their first encounter on neutral ground.[136] E-IMET also funds military participation in overseas conferences, such as the African American Institute's seminar on "The Role of the Military in a Democracy." Although E-IMET funding can be used for these types of overseas initiatives, the program guidelines emphasize training for periods of a longer duration in the United States.

The establishment of the E-IMET program represented a significant policy shift from training foreign militaries solely in lethal tactics or infrastructural development with a by-product of exposure to US culture and values. Instead, E-IMET provides courses and curricula in basic elements of democratic reform. However, several issues of concern remain.

First, surprisingly few E-IMET courses address international human rights and humanitarian law. Only a handful of the course descriptions in the *E-IMET Handbook* explicitly mention human rights. Among them:

- National Security Affairs Curricula (78 weeks);
- Human Rights Instructor Course (3 weeks; taught only in Spanish);
- Civil-Military Strategy for Internal Development (2 weeks); and
- Rule of Law and Disciplined Military Operations (1 week, taught only in Spanish)

Second, according to a National Defense University study on IMET, both the US military services and the foreign aid recipients object to "earmarking" aid toward E-IMET courses. According to the study, it is unlikely that foreign governments and/or their militaries would voluntarily choose E-IMET courses over more traditional military training.

As the RAND Corporation also notes in its study of international military training,

Human rights content in police training

In contrast to several military training programs, US training for foreign law enforcement forces has no mandated requirement for human rights instruction. There may be programs that incorporate such material into training, but not as a matter of policy. The Department of State-funded Antiterrorism Assistance (ATA) program, for example, states in its annual report for FY 2000 that ATA "incorporates a substantial component on democratic law enforcement methods and respect for human rights in its training programs."[137]

A course called "Human Dignity and the Police" was jointly developed by The International Criminal Investigative Training Assistance Program (ICITAP) and CUNY's John Jay College of Criminal Justice in New York. This course has been offered throughout Latin America and the Caribbean, at the International Law Enforcement Academies in Budapest and Bangkok, and also in twenty-two countries in eastern Europe and the former Soviet Union.[138] According to one assessment, "The course begins with police officers' own personal experiences and observations, requires them to develop their own definitions of rights, and takes them through numerous role-playing scenarios. Above all, it seeks to instill a notion of human dignity that is common to all persons, including cops, which should be preserved under all circumstances."[139]

Among the US Federal Bureau of Investigation's international training programs, the one with the most clear human rights content is the International Law Enforcement Academy program in Budapest, which is designed to be similar to the FBI National Academy program in the United States. This program focuses on leadership, human rights, ethics, the rule of law, and other contemporary law enforcement issues.[140] The human rights content of its other programs, including the Mexican/American Law Enforcement Training Initiative and the Pacific Rim Initiative, is not publicly available.

even with the establishment of E-IMET . . . the bulk of
[international military student] training in democratic
ideals, values and institutions will primarily continue to be
the result of incidental exposure [through the voluntary
information program]. Not all international military
students will take E-IMET or theoretical IDAD [internal
defense and development] courses, but they will all be
exposed to US trainers, doctrine and culture, whether in
courses taken in the CONUS [continental United States] or
through some form of MTTs [mobile training teams].[141]

3.3.3. WHINSEC-School of the Americas

US Army Special Forces were training members of the Atlacatl
battalion in El Salvador in the days before and after members of
the battalion killed a woman, her daughter and six Jesuit priests in
November 1989. Three of the four Atlacatl officers implicated had
received some human rights training while attending the Salvadoran
cadet course at the School of the Americas—two officers in 1982 and
one in 1988. Overall, 19 of the 26 soldiers linked to the murder had
taken some training at the SOA. One of them had also attended the
Special Forces Officer Course at Ft. Bragg during late 1988 and
early 1989.[142]

Following the 1989 murders, a dozen protesters led by the Rever-
end Roy Bourgeois launched a vigil at the gates of the School of the
Americas in Ft. Benning, Georgia, pressing for its closure. In the
years since then, what started as a vigil has grown into an effective
reform movement: the SOA Watch Campaign. SOA Watch has helped
publicize numerous revelations about school alumni, who include:

- two of the three officers cited by the Guatemalan archbishop's
  office as suspected directors of the killing of anthropologist Myrna
  Mack in 1992, as well as three high-ranking leaders of the Guatemalan military intelligence unit D-2, including one implicated in
  the 1997 bludgeoning death of Bishop Juan Gerardi.

- two of the three killers of Salvadoran Archbishop Oscar Romero; ten
  of twelve officers responsible for the deaths of 900 civilians in the
  Salvadoran village of El Mozote; Salvadoran death squad leader
  Roberto D'Aubisson; three of the five officers involved in the 1980
  rape and murder of four US church women in El Salvador;

- Manuel Noriega, Panama's former dictator, who was arrested and forcibly extradited by US military forces on drug trafficking charges in 1989;

- Haitian Colonel Gambetta Hyppolite, who ordered his soldiers to fire on an electoral bureau in 1987;

- 123 of the 247 Colombian army officers cited in "El Terrorismo de Estado en Colombia," a 1992 study of human rights abuses in Colombia.[143]

- ten of thirty Chilean officers against whom a Spanish judge sought indictments for crimes of terror, torture and disappearance; and

- Leopoldo Galtieri, former military dictator and a leader of the "dirty war" in Argentina.[144]

SOA Watch also drew public attention to the 1996 disclosure that the School of the Americas had used in courses training manuals advocating execution, torture and blackmail.[145] According to a February 1997 report by the Office of the Inspector General of the Department of Defense, in August 1991 the Secretary of Defense directed the Assistant Secretary of Defense for Intelligence Oversight to investigate the use of the seven Spanish-language manuals, which belatedly had been discovered through an internal review process. Relevant Congressional committees were notified of the discovery in 1991. However, neither the President, Secretary of Defense, Secretary of the Army, the School of the Americas, nor Congress announced the manuals' existence to the public at that time. In fact, when SOA Watch publicized the existence of the manuals in July 1996, the official spokesperson at the School of the Americas denied that such manuals had ever been used.[146] The Pentagon released copies of the manuals two months later, in September 1996.

Several governmental investigations, including those conducted by the Office of the Inspector General of the Department of Defense and the General Accounting Office of the US Congress, found that while the manuals contained improper material, no laws were broken in the preparation, distribution and use of these materials. No one was ever held accountable for the development and use of these manuals, which included twenty-four passages that the Army identified as inconsistent with Army and Department of Defense policy.[147]

Responding to the pressure generated by SOA Watch's revelations, the US House of Representatives twice moved unsuccessfully to close the school. The second attempt, a bill sponsored by Representative Joe Moakley of Massachusetts and 156 other Members of Congress in 1999, noted that SOA was "only part of the United States' extensive training relationship with Latin American armed forces" and that closing the school would not prevent the United States from "providing appropriate training for military personnel of Latin American armed forces." The bill stated, however, that "despite sustained Congressional and public pressure, the United States Army School of the Americas has implemented only limited reforms of its curriculum." In addition to closing the SOA, the bill called for enhanced emphasis on respect for human rights, civil-military relations, and responsible military management through any other IMET or counter-narcotics-funded training provided in the United States, as well as through any training conducted abroad by US Special Forces.

By at vote of 214 to 204, the House narrowly rejected a subsequent amendment to the Defense Authorization Bill for FY 2001 that would have closed the School of the Americas.[148] The US Army presented and Congress passed into law a proposal for several changes at the school, including a new name and a revised legal charter.[149] The Army then announced the "closing" of SOA and reopened the school in January 2001 as the Western Hemisphere Institute for Security Cooperation.

3.3.4 WHINSEC-SOA's human rights program

In response to public outcry over the revelations about SOA's alumni and the use of the training manuals advocating torture, Congress withheld all IMET funding for 1998 until the Secretary of Defense certified that the instruction and training provided by the SOA was "fully consistent with training and doctrine, particularly with respect to the observance of human rights, provided by the Department of Defense to United States military students at Department of Defense institutions whose primary purpose is to train United States military personnel."

In addition, Congress required the Secretary of the Army and the Commander of the US Army Training and Doctrine Command (TRADOC) to confirm to the Secretary of Defense that the Spanish-language material at SOA conformed with US Army doctrine as taught to US and other foreign officers at other TRADOC schools. The Secretary of Defense certified the School of the Americas for two years until the opening of WHINSEC-SOA in early 2001; since then, curriculum review has passed to the Board of Visitors. This board is made up of Members of Congress, military officers, and persons designated by the Secretary of Defense, including, to the extent practicable, individuals from academia and the religious and human rights communities.[150]

Although the Secretary of Defense has certified voluntarily in recent years that the WHINSEC-SOA's teachings are in compliance with US Army doctrine, such accountability is not required by law. Moreover, such certification still does not address the important question of whether US doctrine can be translated well in the context of foreign militaries (see box).

Additional oversight mechanisms include the mostly internal Human Rights Committee at WHINSEC-SOA, which also has a representative from the Bureau of Western Hemisphere Affairs in the Department of State. The mostly external Board of Visitors also provides guidance to the human rights program at WHINSEC-SOA.[151]

A second change, as described above, is the background vetting required for all US taxpayer-funded foreign military training. Security assistance officers (or military groups) in overseas embassies now investigate the human rights, criminal activity and corruption record of all potential foreign military students, except those whose governments pay for their training.

Third, on two separate occasions Congress has required SOA to report on its trainees. Although the Army opposes doing so, it demonstrated in both its 1998 and 2000 reports to Congress that it had some ability to track the school's graduates. As of early 2002, no further reports had been released.

Fourth, a Human Rights and International Law Division has been created in order to manage the school's Human Rights Program. Some changes in the curriculum have also been made in recent years, including the addition of six expanded IMET courses, the development of a peacekeeping course, and some revisions to the commando course that are not publicly known. The two official human rights courses at WHINSEC-SOA are:

- *International Operational Law* (3 weeks): provides instruction on subjects such as the legal basis for the use of force, rules of engagement, civilian law enforcement, human rights, and the role of the military in a democratic society. Includes a minimum of twelve hours in human rights instruction.

- *Human Rights Instructor Course* (3 weeks): seeks "to certify instructors so that they are able to train personnel in the area of human rights back in their own countries." It includes forty hours of human rights instruction on such topics as ethics, the doctrine of just war, the historical development of human rights, and the

US Army doctrine and foreign students

In 1997 the Department of Defense Inspector General (DoD IG) found 24 passages in the SOA field manuals "inconsistent with US policy." These passages, which had been in use for nine years, advocated methods of torture, imprisonment, blackmail, and assassination of noncombatants or detainees.

Other passages in the manuals equated nongovernmental organizations and institutions and other independent voices with subversive or dissident activity. The Army and Department of Defense Inspector General did not find these passages to be inconsistent with US Army doctrine or policy. Much of the rest of these manuals relate to "threat identification and neutralization," which could be seen as advocating human rights abuses, especially if interpreted by an individual lacking knowledge of international humanitarian and customary law. Many of the field manuals with this material continue to be in use today.[152]

Amnesty International USA reviewed one such manual (FM 100-20/ AFP 3-220 Military Operations in Low Intensity Conflict), which referred to "politically neutralizing" targets and developing plans for "the reduction or elimination" of sources of support to targets.[153] US soldiers may know that these terms do not refer to political assassinations, but instead refer to such techniques as radio jamming and effective use of propaganda. Military personnel from governments that tolerate human rights violations, however, may not make such a distinction.

The Defense Security Cooperation Agency failed to respond to Amnesty International USA's inquiries into whether the Department of Defense assesses the relevance or appropriateness of US military doctrine for foreign troops, given differing political histories and contexts.

relationship between human rights and the law of war. Practical exercises, seminars and a case study of the 1968 My Lai Massacre in Vietnam are also integrated into course work.[154]

The number of E-IMET courses offered at WHINSEC-SOA rose from 15 percent of all courses offered in 1996 to 29 percent in 1999[155] and has remained at that level since then. The forty-nine-week Command and General Staff Course (CGSC), which contains a minimum of forty hours of human rights instruction, is considered an E-IMET course, along with Civil Military Operations, Departmental Resource Management, Democratic Sustainment, Human Rights Instructor, and Logistics for Senior Leaders.[156]

Fifth, current WHINSEC-SOA policy is that courses of four-weeks' duration or less include twelve hours of instruction in laws of war and human rights. Courses that run from four weeks to six months include sixteen hours of such instruction, and courses that are longer than six months require 48 hours minimum of human rights instruction.[157] According to US Army Major Tony Raimondo, the human rights content of each course is tailored to the requirements of each course, but basic instruction includes coverage of the American Convention on Human Rights (the Pact of San Jose), international human rights law and international humanitarian law.[158]

Since 1999, SOA (and its successor WHINSEC-SOA) has held an annual "human rights week" during the first week of February, at the beginning of the year-long Command and General Staff Course. Lecturers in 2000 included:

- Hugh Thompson and Larry Colburn, the American soldiers who intervened to stop the massacre at My Lai;

- François Senechaud, an ICRC delegate based in Guatemala, on standards of compliance with International Humanitarian Law; and

- Steven Schneebaum, a human rights lawyer in charge of *pro bono* work at a major Washington, DC law firm, who addressed the enforceability of international human rights law.

A number of these changes were a direct response to pressure from SOA Watch. Many human rights activists remain skeptical of the reforms, however, pointing to a pattern of denials and deceptions surrounding the existence of the torture manuals, a lack of substance in the human rights program, and SOA's prominent display of pictures of infamous SOA graduates, such as the Bolivian dictator General Hugo Benzer, into the early 1990s.

3.4 Operational training and human rights

The majority of foreign military personnel obtaining operational training from the Untied States receive it in combined military exercises. The exercises are usually designed for practicing specific skill sets and operations in the field. With the exception of JCETs, there is no evidence that such exercises includes any sort of human rights or humanitarian law training.[159]

In submitting an annual report on JCET deployments to Congress in 1999, then-Undersecretary of Defense Walter Slocombe asserted that "As we deal with countries struggling to develop democratic institutions, SOF [Special Operations Forces] set an example of professionalism and leadership for those countries by demonstrating a professional military that respects and protects human right and operates under civilian authority and control."[160]

Without such oversight, a fundamental question remains: why should forces whose mission is unconventional warfare—sabotage, psychological operations, working with armed groups and/or paramilitaries—be training, in particular, foreign conventional armies?[161] However, most of the Special Operations doctrine is classified, and many SOF deployments are secret as well. This secrecy makes oversight difficult, if not impossible.

As discussed above, Special Operations Forces deployments abroad for JCETs and other training activities now require a background check of the unit to be trained. Requests for JCET deployments may originate with the US Special Operations Command (USSOCOM), the regional commands, US Ambassadors or the host nation. USSOCOM conducts an annual JCET planning conference, and the Office for Special Operations and Low Intensity Conflict in the Department of Defense submits monthly lists of upcoming JCETs to the Department of State for review. All JCET requests are required to have a human rights review prior to submission to the Joint Staff (which assists the Chairman of the Joint Chiefs of Staff and is composed of officers from the Army, Navy and Marine Corps, and Air

Force). The US Ambassador posted where the exercise is to take place (or the Ambassador's representative), the USSOCOM commander-in-chief, the relevant regional commander-in-chief, and the Secretary of Defense now must review and approve all JCET deployments.

In addition, the Commander of the US Special Operations Command issued a human rights policy memorandum in June 1999. According to this memo, "SOF understand the critical role of human rights in our national security strategy, in USSOCOM's mission, and in the regional CINCs' [commander-in-chiefs'] engagement strategies. Human rights awareness, concepts, reporting requirements and themes will be integrated into all SOF pre-deployment training," with the intention of preventing SOF from training with forces that have committed human rights violations. The statement went on to say that "Promotion of human rights will become a core concept in the education and instruction programs during interactions with the civilian population of the host nation." While the policy memo sounds quite strong in some ways, its use of the future tense should be noted. It is not yet clear how—or whether—this memo translates into operational practice.[162]

In February 2000 Amnesty International USA submitted requests to US Army Special Operations Headquarters at Ft. Bragg, US Special Operations Subcommand of the Central Command, the US European Command, and the US Pacific Command. In all cases, we requested:

- information on pre-deployment human rights training for US troops deploying overseas for any sort of military-to-military contact;

- information on the content and methods used to convey a positive human rights and pro-democracy message to host nation troops; and

- information about whether there have been any reports produced within regional commands of US forces on observations of human rights violations or illegal behavior by host nation troops. Amnesty International USA requested information on whether such reports have been produced, on how the data in the reports went up the chain of command, how the information was conveyed to the host government, and what the outcome was.

The US Southern Command (SOUTHCOM) is the only regional command that indicated an awareness of a human rights policy concerning overseas deployments and training. SOUTHCOM has had a policy on human rights since March 1990, issued by then-commander-in-chief General Maxwell Thurman.[163] The most recent version of the policy, dated July 1, 1998, expresses a strong commitment to human rights and requires

- all US military personnel who enter the Command's area of responsibility (mainland Central and South America) to receive human rights awareness education and to be issued a SOUTHCOM "Human Rights Standing Orders card";

- all US military personnel to "immediately report all instances of suspected violations of internationally recognized human rights through the chain of command to the country's MILGRP commander . . . Allegations . . . will be investigated in coordination with the US Ambassador"; and

- officers and noncommissioned officers in charge of US military personnel deployed to the SOUTHCOM area of responsibility to "include human rights awareness as part of all training provided to allied military forces. All human rights issues and observations will be addressed during initial briefings, periodic training reviews, and after action reports."[164]

As part of pre-deployment preparation, soldiers are shown a ten-minute video featuring General Joulwan, a former commander-in-chief of the Southern Command. In the video, he clearly identifies soldiers' responsibility for recognizing and reporting human rights violations in the Southern Command's theater, and he emphasizes, "the issue is not one of conflict between the mission [of SOUTHCOM] and human rights," but rather that "the mission includes human rights."

3.4.1 Operational training case study: Rwanda

During the genocide of 1994, the Rwandan Armed Forces (FAR) slaughtered between 500,000 and one million Tutsi men, women and children and members of the Hutu community perceived as opponents. Later that year the FAR and its paramilitary allies were defeated by the Rwandan Patriotic Army (RPA), a largely Tutsi force that had defeated and driven out both the FAR and its paramilitary allies. The RPA took control of the devastated country in July 1994. At that time as many as 1.8 million refugees, including individuals who had participated in the genocide, moved across the borders into then-Zaire and Tanzania.

US military re-engagement with Rwanda began in July 1994, when US Special Forces came to Kigali, the capital of Rwanda, in July 1994 to help re-establish the US embassy. Military training began in earnest in 1995, when dozens of Rwandan soldiers and officers were enrolled in expanded IMET courses in the United States. Many of these courses focused on military justice, intended to help meet the enormous need for development of a legal process addressing perpetrators of mass murder. In addition, according to a Pentagon report, US Army Special Forces were deployed to Rwanda beginning in 1995 to train Rwandans in removing landmines.[165] Although there was a clear need for security from attacks by former FAR troops, US Special Operations Forces continued to provide lethal training for the RPA even as RPA units were implicated in mass killings inside Zaire/Democratic Republic of the Congo and Rwanda. Victims of these killings were people whom the RPA suspected of supporting or participating in the genocide.

Amnesty International, Human Rights Watch and the UN field operation established in Rwanda to monitor human rights all documented widespread human rights violations by the RPA. Most abuses took place during large-scale counter-insurgency operations in northwestern Rwanda and former Zaire. According to a report by Amnesty International, the RPA appeared resigned to "the inevitability of occasional casualties in the context of efforts to combat insurgency."[166]

At a hearing in early December 1996, US Representative Chris Smith of New Jersey asked State and Defense Department witnesses whether the US government was providing military training to Rwanda. Ambassador Richard Bogosian, then the State Department's Special Coordinator for Rwanda and Burundi, replied that the United States had "a small IMET program in Rwanda that . . . deals almost exclusively with what you might call the human rights end of the spectrum as distinct from purely military operations. There is no substantial military assistance at the moment."

Vincent Kern, then-Deputy Assistant Secretary of Defense for African Affairs, added: "We are talking about the softer, kinder, gentler side of the military training, focusing on improving skills in areas such as civil/military relations, the role of the military in civilian society, those sorts of programs. We have not provided Rwanda with any of the sort of basic military training that you would get at Ft. Bragg officer training, those sorts of things."[167]

In fact, Ft. Bragg had come to Kigali five months prior to that testimony. Representative Smith later found out that a detachment from the 3rd Special Forces Group (airborne) had trained thirty-five to forty Rwandan troops in a JCET exercise called "Falcon Gorilla" in Rwanda during July and August 1996. Documents subsequently released to Representative Smith clearly show the mission as training to plan and conduct Foreign Internal Defense (FID), or counterinsurgency. "The primary objective of this training is to satisfy mission letter requirements in FID skills and enhance professional development through training host nation forces . . . to train, assist and advise selected RPA junior officers and NCOs in light infantry skills and staff procedures necessary to plan, resource and sustain both training and operations." These skills included basic rifle marksmanship, commando tactics, night land navigation and small unit tactics.[168]

Although the documents released do indicate the careful nature of SOF training—including battery support requests, hazardous cargo lists and order forms for trainee graduation certificates—they include a JCET program of instruction calendar with advanced marksmanship scheduled for August 9th and ambush organization planning scheduled for August 17th.

To fend off Congressional criticism, the Pentagon prepared in 1998 a summary report of US military activities in Rwanda from the end of the 1994 genocide until August 1997. According to this report, the first JCET exercise ("Falcon Gorilla") was held from July 15 to August 30, 1996. The following year, Army Special Forces taught "Civil Affairs" via a mobile training team in Rwanda, and a second JCET exercise was held, again from July 15 to August 30. This exercise focused on leadership development. In addition, two Rwandan Patriotic Army officers attended "Civil Military Strategy for International Development" at the Air Force Special Operations headquarters at Hurlbert Field, Florida during July and August 1997. This course is considered an E-IMET program. The report provides no specific units or designations of the Rwandan forces that received training in these venues.[169]

It is unclear whether the Pentagon's civilian leadership and the State Department's coordinator for regional policy were aware in December 1996 that a JCET exercise involving lethal combat skills had occurred six months earlier. The exercise took place in a "hot" conflict zone where many human rights violations were reported. This exercise led Congress to require in 1998 that the Secretary of Defense personally give prior approval to all future JCET exercises.

In summer 1998, Pentagon spokeswoman Colonel Nancy Burt said that "as a practical matter, it would not be feasible" to vet Rwandan forces being trained through the JCET program for prior human rights violations "due to the large number of persons with whom we conduct training."[170] Subsequently, such a requirement was enacted into law, and the Pentagon appears to be making an effort to comply.

In 1997 the Rwandan Patriotic Army launched large-scale military operations in response to attacks by armed groups in western Rwanda (principally by former FAR and allied Hutu militias from Zaire). According to the United Nations Human Rights Field Operation (HFOR) in Rwanda, in May and June 1997 more than 2,000 people were killed during RPA operations in the northwestern provinces of Rwanda. "HFOR has gathered, analyzed and cross-checked information showing a high number of killings during the cordon and search operations, including a reportedly high number of unarmed civilians, such as elderly persons, women and young children," the UN office reported.[171]

In 1997 Representative Smith requested the names of all Rwandan troops trained in JCET exercises since 1994, as well as after-action reports from the training missions. The Pentagon never provided him with this information. In the absence of such information from the US government, it has not been possible to correlate forces that received IMET, JCET or landmine removal training from the US military with abuses in Rwanda or Zaire/Democratic Republic of the Congo.

Attacks on noncombatant civilians continue. In a May 2000 study on the war in the Democratic Republic of the Congo, Human Rights Watch reported that Rwanda and its allies "have regularly slaughtered civilians in massacres and extrajudicial executions."[172]

The "Disappeared"

December 25, 1997. Médard Gashumba, a medical assistant, was arrested, detained in the *cachot* (local detention center) at Gabiro in Rwanda and released later the same day. On December 26, RPA soldiers came to his house, shot him dead and reportedly removed his body from the scene. His wife Perpétue, his four-year-old daughter Liliane Ingabire and two servants were led away and never seen again. It is presumed that they too were killed. Neither the body of Médard Gashumba nor those of his wife, daughter and servants have been found.

January 9, 1998. RPA soldiers took Juvénal Bagarirakose to an unknown destination from his home commune of Kibilira, the site of intense violence, in Gisenyi. The soldiers reportedly burned the nearby houses of two of his sisters before leaving the area. Amnesty International knows of no official acknowledgement that Juvénal Bagarirakose's was arrested or "disappeared," and fears he is dead. A teacher by training who had also worked in the commercial sector, Juvénal Bagarirakose was married with three children. He had been a refugee in the former Zaire between 1994 and November 1996, when he returned to Rwanda. While a refugee, he was involved in initiatives to promote dialogue and non-violent solutions to the conflict in Rwanda. He continued to pursue these activities following his return to Rwanda, taking an active role in discussion and prayer groups with Hutu and Tutsi communities with the full knowledge and the cooperation of local civilian authorities.[173]

3.4.2 Operational training case study: Indonesia

Sixteen-year-old Levi Corte-Real Bucar was one of hundreds of young people who attended the peaceful pro-independence rally at the Santa Cruz cemetery in Dili, East Timor, on November 12, 1991. He remained at the entrance of the cemetery and recounts how the Indonesian army began shooting at the unarmed demonstrators: "They shot us straightaway. I was in the front row and fell to the ground to avoid the bullets. I saw two of my friends bleeding profusely, dying. I thought, 'I'm going to die too.' A bullet had entered my back, and I lost consciousness." The next thing Levi says that he remembers is Indonesian soldiers walking among the bodies and looking for survivors. "One came to me. He had his bayonet in his hand. He said to me, 'Get up!' When I stood, he stabbed me five times." Levi was fortunate enough to be taken to a hospital, where he eventually recovered from his physical wounds; others were not so lucky. An estimated 271 people were killed, 278 wounded, 103 hospitalized and 270 "disappeared" during the Santa Cruz Massacre.[174]

In response to the massacre, Congress cut off IMET funding for Indonesia in 1992. From 1950 until the cutoff, the US government had paid for the training of more than 7,300 Indonesian officers at US-based Army, Navy, and Air Force schools. Despite the fact that Congressional sponsors of the 1992 action had made it clear that they intended to cut off *all* Indonesian armed forces access to US military training, some training continued. The Indonesian government purchased through the Foreign Military Sales (FMS) program the same types of training provided through IMET.

In 1995 a majority in Congress yielded to strong pressure by the Clinton Administration for re-engagement with the Indonesian armed forces and supported funding for E-IMET courses on civil-military relations. The Administration justified the engagement on grounds of the country's strategic location and demographics. Indonesia has the fourth largest population in the world and is the world's largest Muslim country. From a dozen to twenty Indonesian officers attended E-IMET courses annually, with funding from the US government, beginning in 1996.

In September 1997, Representative Lane Evans of Illinois requested information on all US military training relations with Indonesia. He received a reply from the Pentagon in April 1998 that focused on professional military courses taken in the United States— i.e., courses purchased via IMET or FMS.

The following month, the East Timor Action Network (ETAN) revealed that US Air Force, Army and Navy Special Forces had used the JCET program to provide training to Indonesian Special Forces units throughout the period of the ban imposed by Congress on operational, lethal training. Thirty-six JCET exercises had taken place in Indonesia from 1992 to May 8, 1998, when publication of an exposé by reporter and ETAN activist Allan Nairn brought training to a halt.[175]

Nairn's allegations were later confirmed by the Pentagon, which disclosed that training routinely included sniper techniques, air assault operations, amphibious operations, and close quarters combat techniques. In addition to these exercises, US Special Forces deployed to Indonesia twice during 1995 and 1996 on classified missions.

ETAN and Representative Evans also revealed that US Marine Corps expeditionary forces and reconnaissance groups had been holding annual training exercises with Indonesian Armed Forces since 1992. The annual "deployment for training" exercises are known as Force Reconnaissance Exercise (FORECONEX) and Cooperation Afloat Readiness and Training (CARAT). Training included small arms weapons instruction, demolition classes, ambush skills and squad level attacks.[176]

In April 1998 Representative Evans requested detailed information from the Pentagon specifically on US Special Forces and Marine Corps training programs with Indonesian forces. The Deputy Secretary of Defense responded in mid-July 1998, just as *The Washington Post* was concluding a three-day series of articles on the JCET program, stating, "All Department of Defense bilateral activities with Indonesia have been conducted in accordance with the law."[177]

This claim was technically true, as Congress had not legally proscribed any forms of assistance except IMET. Moreover, the Department of Defense had been reporting annually to Congress on JCET exercises held in Indonesia and elsewhere. Nevertheless, this training occurred during the Indonesian military's violent repression of the pro-independence movement in East Timor. The United Nations and most governments recognized that East Timor was illegally occupied by Indonesian forces. Moreover, the Pentagon downplayed the role of JCET and Marine Corps training in Indonesia, even after Congress expressed concern over such programs in the context of Rwanda.

In his response to Representative Evans, the Deputy Secretary of Defense noted that, again, the US government could not name the soldiers whom it had trained. "The US government does not request the host nation to provide the records of individual service members who would participate in training with US forces," he wrote, stating that the highest level of detail possible is the name of the service that was trained.

In 1997 Representative Nita Lowey of New York requested detailed information from the State and Defense Departments on Indonesian military personnel who had received IMET and E-IMET training in the United States, including their names and rank. The Department of Defense complied for the period of 1987 to 1997, providing information for courses taken in all US military schools, whether paid for with IMET grant aid or purchased with Indonesian funds through the FMS program. An analysis of this information prepared by Amnesty International USA's analysis of this information in 1998 found only one clear connection between the list of trainees and human rights violations.[178] In addition, Lt. General Prabowo Subianto, the former head of Kopassus (Special Forces Command), received American military training. Kopassus is an elite combat unit of the Indonesian military that has been responsible for some of the worst violations in Indonesia's history.

The violence in Indonesia escalated in late August 1999, when balloting to determine the future of East Timor was to take place. Supporters of independence in East Timor were targeted by pro-Indonesian militias set up and supported by the Indonesian military. After August 1999 President Clinton cut off all arms sales and other military ties to Indonesia. This action and other pressure led to the Indonesian government's acceptance of a Security Council-sanctioned military force that was to restore peace and security in East Timor, protect and support the United Nations Assistance Mission to East Timor (UNAMET), and assist in the facilitation of humanitarian operations. The US Administration, however, re-established funding for a small number of Indonesian officers to take E-IMET courses in FY 2001, and Congress supported this request.[179] Meanwhile, Indonesia has not taken effective steps to disband the East Timorese militia groups, which are now based in West Timor, Indonesia. In September 2000 members of these militias were responsible for the murder of three United Nations High Commissioner for Refugees (UNHCR) officials. Militia harassment and intimidation of East Timorese refugees in West Timor continues to be reported, while plans move forward on the re-engagement of US and Indonesian military forces in training exercises.

3.4.3 Operational training case study: Colombia

Reportedly in response to the bomb explosion on an Avianca passenger jet with several Americans on board, President George H.W. Bush ordered an unprecedented training program for the Colombian National Police (CNP) in 1992. Pablo Escobar, the notorious leader of the Medellin Cartel, was believed to be behind the bombing, which killed all aboard. Under orders from the President, then-US Ambassador to Colombia Morris Busby "turned the US embassy into a war command," according to reporter Mark Bowden's newspaper series "Killing Pablo," and dispatched a team of Marine Corps trainers to form a small army of 120 men within the CNP. This unit was modeled after the US Delta Force: direct action forces honed to go anywhere on a moment's notice and conduct a wide range of operations. Their mission was to wipe out the Colombian drug cartels and, in particular, Pablo Escobar.

According to a CBS "60 Minutes" interview, former Marine Major Gil Macklin, who headed up part of the training project, trained the CNP unit to "kill or be killed." These forces killed nearly 100 lieutenants in Escobar's private army of mercenaries before finally cornering Escobar and killing him in December 1993.[180]

In the month-long series entitled "Killing Pablo," published in *The Philadelphia Inquirer* in November 2000, investigative reporter Mark Bowden revealed that members of an elite US military training team were sharing intelligence with members of the PEPES (People Persecuted by Pablo Escobar), a death squad that set out in 1993 to attack and destroy anyone associated with Pablo Escobar. The articles point to other forms of collaboration with PEPES and missed opportunities to arrest the former leader of the group, Fidel Castaño, who was wanted on charges of terrorism.

Following Escobar's death, PEPES became a nationwide para-military network directed against Colombia's opposition movements and people believed to support them. Carlos Castaño, the brother of Fidel, heads this paramilitary network. Known as the United Self-Defense Forces of Colombia (AUC), these paramilitaries

"They cannot kill everyone"

On May 25, 2000, 26-year-old reporter Jineth Bedoya Lima went to a Bogota-area prison to interview an AUC paramilitary leader about rumors that she was on his "hit list." While waiting for the interview, Bedoya was kidnapped at gunpoint, drugged, then brutally beaten and repeatedly raped by her captors. That evening a taxi driver found her in a garbage dump, where she had been left with her hands bound.

As a journalist for *El Espectador,* a daily newspaper in Bogota, Colombia, Bedoya Lima covers the conflict between the Colombian government and paramilitary groups. She has been harassed and has received death threats because of her reporting. Although many Colombian journalists have fled for their lives after repeated threats, Bedoya returned to her job just two weeks after being abducted. She has decided to stay in Colombia and continue reporting, although she now does so with the protection of a bodyguard. As she says, "They can silence me and kill me and torture me, but there will always be someone willing to expose the truth. And they cannot kill everyone."[181]

are responsible for the vast majority of political killings in Colombia in recent years.

Amnesty International USA began investigating possible collusion between US government agencies and Colombian death squads in 1994. Documents obtained under the Freedom of Information Act make it clear that the US Embassy was aware of numerous terror attacks, including bombings and murders, carried out by PEPES at the height of their collaboration with the US in 1993. Moreover, Fidel Castaño was known to be a drug trafficker, as acknowledged in a 1993 Defense Intelligence Agency Counterdrug Division document.[182]

As a result of *The Philadelphia Inquirer* series, several Members of Congress wrote to then-President Clinton in late 2000, urging him to convene an Intelligence Oversight Board to review "the role of US agencies and the relationship of US agencies, both direct and indirect, with the Colombian group Los Pepes."[183] The President is not known to have initiated the investigation before leaving office.

Meanwhile, Colombia continues to suffer a human rights emergency, with more than 3,700 people killed or "disappeared" in 2001, mostly at the hands of the paramilitary groups. Up to 347,000 were displaced within Colombia in 2001, and more than 3,000 were kidnapped by guerrilla or paramilitary groups. While the Colombian government has outlawed paramilitary groups, military and para-military forces continue to operate in extensive collusion, both tacitly and actively. The paramilitaries operate in heavily militarized areas, managing to pass through Colombian military roadblocks with no interference from the army. Frequently, serious human rights violations are committed against civilians in joint military-paramilitary operations.

Killings in Mapiripán, Colombia on July 20, 1997, raise questions about whether the US military continued to provide indirect but close, support to the paramilitaries beyond the era of the PEPES. Several dozen people were taken from their homes, tortured and murdered in Mapiripán that day. The AUC took responsibility for the deaths.[184] Just prior to and after the killings, the US Army 7th Special Forces Group trained Colombian forces at the Colombian Army Special Forces School at El Barrancón, near the town of Mapiripán. Among the trainees were units of the Colombian Army's 2nd Mobile Brigade, which has a history of human rights abuses. The brigade was headed at the time by Colonel Lino Hernando Sanchez Prado, who was dismissed from the army in 2001 and is now under investi-gation by judicial authorities in connection with the killings.

A detailed investigation published in the Colombian newspaper *El Espectador* in February 2000 concluded that the US Army Special Operations 7th Group (Green Berets) carried out "military planning" training with Colonel Sanchez's troops at the time he was planning the killings.[185] In a much delayed response to this report, the US government asserted that Colonel Lino Sanchez definitely *did not* receive training from US Special Forces at the military school, nor were personnel at the school under his command.[186]

In February 2001, after pressure from human rights monitors for accountability in the Mapiripán case, a military court convicted General Jaime Uscategui of failing to stop the killings. Uscategui was removed as commander of the army's 7th Brigade soon after the deaths, and he received a sentence of forty months in prison. He was acquitted of homicide charges.[187]

Meanwhile, in 2000 and 2001, the United States Congress approved "Plan Colombia," allocating $750 million in new military training and equipment for the Colombian armed forces and Colombian National Police. US Special Forces deployed to Colombia in January 2001 to train the third of three specialized anti-drug battalions created with this aid under "Plan Colombia." The US Southern Command has acknowledged that the skills conveyed through "light infantry counter-drug trainings" are "equally applicable to counter-insurgent operations."[188]

For Fiscal Year 2003, the Bush Administration seeks $439 million for Colombia under the Andean Counterdrug Initiative (ACI), which sustains and expands programs from Plan Colombia. In addition to providing funds for social and economic programs, ACI also would enable Colombia to set up a second counter-drug brigade. Two additional brigades of the Colombian armed forces will be trained and equipped with $98 million in Foreign Military Financing funds, which will help the Colombian government protect the Cano Limon-Covenas oil pipeline from guerrilla attacks.[189]

4
Priority areas for action

Based on the findings of this report, Amnesty International USA recommends that the US government:

1. **Increase transparency and accountability of the training provided to foreign militaries.** AIUSA's research suggests that operational military training is at times provided to foreign forces, which can reasonably be assumed to contribute to human rights violations in some instances. In the case studies in this report, such information came to light largely as a result of concerted campaigns by nongovernmental organizations. Such transparency and account-ability to the US public and US Congress should not be left to chance.

- **The US Congress should enact the Human Rights Information Act and the Foreign Military Training Responsibility Act** to release information on past military, security and police training and other military operations, including covert training, where persistent, widespread or grave human rights violations have occurred and to address current oversight, accountability and transparency shortfalls.

- **The US Department of Defense should disclose publicly information about Joint Combined Exchange Training (JCETs) and other such training deployments with foreign troops, disclosing where Special Operations Forces units trained, with whom, and the type of training they provided.** With the exception of Congressional queries, the Department of Defense is currently not forthcoming in providing public information about operational training programs, particu-larly involving Special Operations Forces. Even many Members of Congress are not privy to details.

- **The US Congress should require the State Department to include monitoring and public disclosure provisions in export licenses granted to private military companies or as a condition for any contracts with private military companies for training of foreign militaries.** This could include an annual report listing which private companies have been authorized to do what, where, for whom and for what duration. This legislative requirement should also mandate that overseas embassies monitor the conduct of these private training programs. In addition, to provide better oversight, Congress should require the Department of State to notify Congress of all potential licenses for the provision of operational military training by private contractors at least thirty days prior to the granting of an export license for such training.

- **The US Congress should require the Departments of Defense and State to include in the annual report on *Foreign Military Training and DoD Engagement Activities of Interest* information about foreign military forces' home unit and the location of training received in the United States.** The Defense Security Cooperation Agency, the agency that compiles the report, has justified withholding such information from the US public as necessary to protect the privacy and security of foreign military officers who come to the United States to train. Such concerns should not outweigh compliance with US law and foreign policy.

- **In weighing which information to include in the annual report on *Foreign Military Training and DoD Engagement Activities of Interest,* the US Department of Defense and the US Department of State need to place greater importance on the public's right to know.** The US Congress should require a written justification from the US Department of Defense or the US Department of State for the classification or withholding of information previously released to the public in the 1998–1999 version of this report.

2. **Strengthen background vetting of trainees.** The Leahy Law requiring background screening of trainees has been expanded since its introduction in 1996 to cover most forms of US government-financed military and police training. While the Departments of State and Defense have made considerable progress in implementing this law, several areas of concern remain.

- **The US Congress should require that Leahy Law background screenings apply not only to training funded through US government grants or loans, but also to**

training purchased by foreign governments. The majority of foreign military training provided by the United States is purchased with foreign states' own funds, with no requirement for background checks of trainees.

- **The US Congress should require that Leahy Law background investigations apply to international police training programs run by the US Federal Bureau of Investigation (FBI).** The FBI's training of foreign police and security forces is funded from the US Justice Department's budget, which the Leahy provision technically does not cover. This situation should be clarified and remedied with legislation if necessary.

- **The US Congress should require staff in US Embassies to contact national and international human rights organizations when reviewing potential military students' backgrounds where appropriate.** In some cases, local or international nongovernmental organizations may have information that can be used in conducting background checks. Currently, Embassy staffs are not required to seek or report such information.

- **The US Congress should require the US Departments of State and Defense to include in the annual report on *Foreign Military Training and DoD Engagement Activities of Interest* information on the implementation of US law related to background screenings for human rights.** In particular, the report should establish and verify that vetting procedures are consistent from embassy to embassy. The report should also include records on units and individuals trained through the JCET program.

- **The US Secretary of State should direct US Ambassadors to notify host governments of any evidence they discover in the process of conducting background checks that potential training candidates are implicated in past human rights violations.**

- **The US Congress should extend follow-up monitoring now required for International Military Education and Training (IMET) program recipients to all foreign recipients of US military training, and provide the resources necessary**

for implementation. The October 2000 legislation setting up a tracking system for all recipients of IMET funds should be standard practice, not just for WHINSEC-SOA students and IMET recipients, but for all foreign military trainees.

- **The US Congress should provide additional funding in the annual State Department appropriations** in order to adequately staff the additional reporting and tracking requirements.

3. Mainstream human rights and humanitarian law education into all foreign military training.

- **The US military should integrate human rights and humanitarian law into all training courses at US-based military institutions that include foreign military, security and police personnel. This instruction should be mandatory for all US and foreign trainees attending courses, and it should be reinforced through operational training exercises.** Currently, for the great majority of foreign military trainees, no such instruction is required. WHINSEC-SOA's core human rights program or the Investigative Criminal Investigative Training and Assistance Program's (ICITAP) partnership with John Jay College could serve as models for some 275 US institutions providing training to foreign military and law enforcement officers.

- **The US Departments of State and Defense should evaluate existing expanded IMET (E-IMET) courses and promote and encourage the development of more specialized and intensive E-IMET courses with additional explicit human rights and international humanitarian law focus.** The civilian leadership of the Departments of State and Defense must ensure that "earmarking" of US military aid toward E-IMET courses is not criticized by the US armed services training with foreign militaries, thereby undermining the intent and value of the E-IMET program.

4. Provide more oversight of US training provided to foreign militaries.

- **The US Department of State should develop a more coordinated system for allocating military, security and**

police training to foreign governments. In particular, the US Department of State should make a considered policy decision about what kind of training is appropriate for each recipient nation taking into account the political-military and law enforcement context of the recipient nation; the human rights situation, particularly if there is active armed conflict; and US law and foreign policy.

- **The US Department of State should also provide oversight of and policy guidance for the use of US Special Operations Forces (SOF) for training of foreign forces, especially training involving regular (conventional) forces.** Given the nature of SOF missions, it is especially important that such training be reconciled with US law and foreign policy, as well as the political-military and human rights context of the recipient nation.

5. **Investigate and suspend the School of the Americas/WHINSEC and introduce strong human rights safeguards in all US military, security and police training schools.** Although the United States Army claims that it has closed the School of the Americas (SOA) and established the Western Hemisphere Institute for Security Cooperation (WHINSEC) as an entirely new institution that happens to be located in the same physical space, WHINSEC is essentially the same school as SOA, with the same primary mission—conveying military skills to members of Latin American armed forces.

- Over the past decade, sustained public and US Congressional pressure on WHINSEC-SOA has resulted in several reforms, including greater external oversight, additional public reporting, and expanded human rights education content. However, the United States should recognize and acknowledge that the school's history places a particularly heavy burden on the US Army to ensure that the "new" institution and all other US military, security and police training schools are transparent and that these schools, their students and their graduates are accountable for any future human rights abuses. In that spirit, **the US government should make it a general condition that all future students and graduates accepted for US military, security**

67

and police training will only gain entry if their home state has established effective laws and regulations that ensure accountability should they commit any human rights abuses in the future.

- To help further prevent abuses, **the United States Congress should adopt legislation that would require the Secretary of Defense to review and certify that all US military, security and police courses and training manuals are consistent with US obligations under international human rights and humanitarian law.** For the past several years, the Secretary of Defense has conducted the review on a voluntary basis of the WHINSEC-SOA materials, but such a transparency and confidence-building measure should not depend on the goodwill of the Secretary of Defense.

- **The US Congress also should require the Department of Defense to assess and report annually on all US military, security and police training schools' progress in integrating human rights and rule of law education into military training.** The same report also should examine whether the independent investigation into WHINSEC-SOA's past practices and reforms can be applied in a systemic fashion to other US training of foreign militaries, making human rights coursework the rule rather than an exception.

- In addition, changes to the WHINSEC-SOA institution and its curriculum do not absolve the US government of responsibility for identifying and prosecuting those responsible for past human rights violations perpetrated by the School of the Americas, including past and current US Army officials responsible for having drafted, approved, or taught with manuals that advocate illegal tactics such as torture. **The US government should take immediate steps to establish an independent commission to investigate the past activities of the SOA and its graduates, particularly the use of these manuals in SOA training and the impact of such training.** The independent commission should also examine the activities of all other US military, security and training schools and make recommendations to establish safeguards to prevent violations of international human rights and humanitarian law. It should examine whether particular reparations are necessary for the victims of such violations and in particular work with the US Department of Justice to hold accountable those responsible for making the United States complicit in human rights violations abroad as a result of the training of and support for SOA students and graduates.

- **Pending the publication of the findings of the above-mentioned independent commission of inquiry, training at the WHINSEC-SOA should be suspended.** Not establishing strict accountability in this instance would send the signal that military impunity (in this case within the US Army) is permissible. This would be unacceptable from a government that sees itself as an advocate of human rights and a school that has sought to portray itself as teaching military responsibility and human rights.

- **The independent commission of inquiry should recommend appropriate reparations for any violations of human rights to which training at SOA contributed, including criminal prosecutions, redress for victims and their families, and a public apology.**

Appendix 1

Partial listing of military institutions in the United States providing training for foreign military students, by state

Alabama

US Army Ordnance, Missile and Munitions Center and School,
     Redstone Arsenal
US Army Aviation Center, Ft Rucker
US Army School of Aviation Medicine, Ft Rucker
Air Command and Staff College, Maxwell AFB, AL
Ira C. Eaker College for Professional Development, Maxwell AFB
US Army Military Police School, Ft McClellan
Coast Guard Aviation Training Center, Mobile

Arizona

US Army Intelligence Center and School, Ft Huachuca
Western Army National Guard Aviation Training Site, Marana
Marine Corps Air Station, Yuma

California

US Army National Training Center, Ft Irwin
Naval Postgraduate School, Monterey
Defense Resources Management Institute, Monterey
Expeditionary Warfare Training Group, Pacific, San Diego
Helicopter Combat Support Squadron Three, Naval Air Station
     North Island, San Diego
Fleet Anti-Submarine Warfare Training Center San Diego
Naval Construction Training Center, Port Hueneme
Naval Special Warfare Command, Coronado
Marine Corps Air Base, West Miramar
Marine Corps Base, Camp Pendleton
Marine Corps Mountain Warfare Training Center, Bridgeport
Marine Corps Air Ground Combat Center, Twentynine Palms
Coast Guard Training Center, Petaluma

Pacific Area, US Coast Guard, Alameda

Colorado
US Air Force Academy, Colorado Springs

Connecticut
Navy Submarine School, Groton
Coast Guard Academy, New London

Washington, DC
Walter Reed Army Medical Center
Armed Forces Institute of Pathology
National Defense University, Ft McNair
National War College, Ft McNair
Center for Hemispheric Studies, Ft McNair
Defense Intelligence Agency
Central Intelligence Agency

Florida
Air Force Special Operations School, Hurlburt Field
Commodore Training Air Wing Five, Milton
USAF Detachment 2, 361st Training Squadron, Naval Air Station,
    Pensacola
Naval Aviation Schools Command, Naval Air Station, Pensacola
Navy OPMEDINST, Pensacola
Navy Technical Training Center, Corry Station, Pensacola
Naval School, Explosive Ordnance Disposal, Eglin AFB
Naval Diving and Salvage Training Center, Panama City
Helicopter Anti-Submarine Warfare Wing, US Atlantic Fleet Naval Air
    Station, Jacksonville
Seventh Coast Guard District, Miami

Georgia

US Army School of the Americas/Western Hemisphere Institute for
    Security Cooperation, Ft Benning
US Army Infantry School, Ft Benning
US Army Signal Center, Ft Gordon
Dwight D. Eisenhower Army Medical Center, Ft Gordon

US Army Forces Command, Ft McPherson
Navy Supply Corps School, Athens
Marine Corps Logistics Bases, Albany

Hawaii
Tripler Army Medical Center, Honolulu
Navy Submarine Training Center, Pacific, Pearl Harbor
Fourteenth Coast Guard District, Honolulu
Asia-Pacific Center, Honolulu

Illinois
US Army Management Engineering College, Rock Island

Kansas
US Army Command and General Staff College Ft Leavenworth

Kentucky
US Army Armor School, Ft Knox

Louisiana
Eighth Coast Guard District, New Orleans

Massachusetts
First Coast Guard District, Boston

Maryland
US Naval Academy, Annapolis
Defense Information School, Ft Meade
United States Naval Test Pilot School, Naval Air Station, Patuxent

Missouri
US Army Engineer Center, Ft Leonard Wood
US Army Chemical School, Ft Leonard Wood
Marine Corps Detachment, Ft Leonard Wood

Mississippi
Navy Technical Training Center, Meridian

Naval Construction Training Center, Gulfport
81st Training Group, Keesler AFB

North Carolina

US Army JFK Special Warfare Center and School, Ft Bragg
18th Airborne Corps, Ft Bragg
Navy Small Craft Instruction and Technical Training School,
    Camp LeJeune
Marine Corps Base, Camp LeJeune
Marine Corps Air Base, East, Cherry Point
Marine Corps Air Station, New River

New Mexico

49th Fighter Wing Training Squadron, Holloman AFB
542nd Crew Training Wing, Kirtland AFB

Nevada

57th Fighter Wing, Nellis AFB

New York

US Military Academy, West Point

Ohio

Defense Institute of Security Assistance Management,
    Wright-Patterson AFB

Oklahoma

US Army Defense Ammunition Center, McAlester
US Army Field Artillery School, Ft Sill

Pennsylvania

US Army War College, Carlisle Barracks
Naval Supply Systems Command, Mechanicsburg
Eastern US Army National Guard Aviation Training Site, Annville
Naval Inventory Control Point, Naval Support Station, Philadelphia

Rhode Island

Naval War College, Newport

Naval Justice School, Newport
Surface Warfare Officers School Command, Newport

South Carolina
US Army Training Center, Ft Jackson

Texas
US Army Medical Department Center and School, Ft Sam Houston
US Army Air Defense Artillery School, Ft Bliss
US Army Sergeants Major Academy, Ft Bliss
US Army Medical Department Center School, Ft Sam Houston
21st Cavalry Brigade (Air Combat), Ft Hood
USAF School of Aerospace Medicine, Brooks AFB
Defense Language Institute English Language Center, Lackland AFB
Inter-American Air Forces Academy, Lackland AFB
International Office, 82nd Airborne, Sheppard AFB
12th Flying Training Wing, Randolph AFB
47th Flying Training Wing, Laughlin AFB
315th Training Squadron, Goodfellow AFB
Mine Warfare Training Center, Ingleside

Virginia
USA Logistics Management College, Ft Lee
USA Transportation School 765 Battalion, Ft Eustis
US Army Logistics Management College, Ft Lee
US Army Aviation Logistics School, Ft Eustis
US Army Judge Advocate General School, Charlottesville
Defense Mapping School, Ft Belvoir
Naval Special Warfare Development Group, Dam Neck
Joint Forces Staff College, Norfolk
Expeditionary Warfare Training Group, Atlantic, Northfolk
US Marine Corps General Command and Staff College, Quantico
US Marine Corps Combat Development Command, Quantico
US Marine Corps Scout Sniper Instruction School, Quantico
Fleet Combat Training Center, Norfolk
374th Training Wing Detachment, Portsmouth
Coast Guard Reserve Training Center, Yorktown
Coast Guard Atlantic Area, Portsmouth

Washington

9th Infantry Division, Ft Lewis

Navy Undersea Warfare Center, Keyport

Madigan Army Medical Center, Tacoma

Coast Guard National Motor Lifeboat School, Ilwaco

Thirteenth Coast Guard District, Seattle

Appendix 2

Methodology and acknowledgments

Lora Lumpe, an independent expert on military issues, initiated this study in mid-December 1999. Leslie Smith, a research assistant for Amnesty International USA, and Sharon Burke, Advocacy Director for the Middle East and North Africa, provided additional research and editorial services. The report is derived from interviews and documents gathered from a number of collegial organizations. AIUSA gratefully acknowledges the assistance through materials, dialogue or feedback of Joy Olson and Lisa Haugaard of the Latin America Working Group; Carole Richardson of SOA Watch; Adam Isacson of the Center for International Policy; Rachel Nield of the Washington Office on Latin America; Lynn Fredricksson of the East Timor Action Network; Tamar Gabelnick, Steven Aftergood and Keith Tidball of the Federation of American Scientists; Dana Priest of *The Washington Post*; Michael McClintock and Bill Arkin of Human Rights Watch; Jim Cason of *La Jornada*; Kate Doyle of the National Security Archives; Nicole Ball of the Overseas Development Council; Samina Ahmed of the Kennedy School of Government, Harvard University; Deborah Avant of George Washington University; Peter Batchelor, Centre on Conflict Resolution, University of Capetown; and Adotei Akwei, Maureen Greenwood, T. Kumar and Andrew Miller at Amnesty International USA. Special thanks to Carlos Salinas, former Acting Legislative Director at AIUSA, and Alex Arriaga, the current Director of Government Relations at AIUSA.

In March 2000 and April 2001, interim drafts of this report were circulated within AIUSA to staff, managers, country specialists, and the MSP working group. The MSP working group again reviewed a draft in March 2002, and AIUSA acknowledges the valuable insight and input from the Chair, Susan Waltz, and the members, Diego Zavala, Bill Godnick, Sarah Milburn, Meredith Larson, Lora Lumpe, and Sean McFate. The drafts were also submitted to the Amnesty's International Secretariat, with Michael Crowley and Brian Wood serving as point persons. A good deal of valuable feedback and inputs were received from all. Thank you.

Several requests for information were filed under the Freedom of Information Act, and some were fulfilled—most notably a major request for information from the US Army School of the Americas. Others are still pending with the Office of the Secretary of Defense.

In addition, personal or telephone interviews were held with officials of the US Army, the School of the Americas, Office of the Secretary of Defense, Office of the Assistant Secretary of Defense for Special Operations and Low Intensity Conflict, the National Defense University, each of the unified regional commands, the Special Operations Command, Ft. Bragg, the Bureaus of Western Hemisphere Affairs and African Affairs at the US Department of State, and the US Agency for International Development, as well as Members of Congress and their staff. Some of these sources requested that their names and titles not be disclosed in the report.

All web links and citations are valid as of March 2002.

Endnotes

1 Testimony of a 15-year-old girl who was repeatedly raped in her house in Kabul in March 1994. Taken from Amnesty International's publication *Afghanistan: International Responsibility for Human Rights Disaster*, November 1995.

2 US Department of State, "Background Notes: Afghanistan," July 1994.

3 Anthony Beilenson, "Cut Off Aid to the Afghan Rebels," *The New York Times*, May 22, 1989, submitted into Congressional Record by Representative Don Edwards on May 25, 1989; see also Rosanne Klass, "United States Must Reassess Afghan Policy," *Wall Street Journal*, October 18, 1989, submitted into Congressional Record by Senator Gordon Humphrey on October 20, 1989.

4 *The Economist*, "A Bitter Harvest," September 13, 2001.

5 Amnesty International, *Afghanistan: International Responsibility for Human Rights Disaster*, November 1995.

6 Remarks by Representative David Dreier in the House of Representatives on July 24, 1990; he stated: "Led by Ritter, nineteen members of Congress have written a series of letters to President Bush in recent months asking why the United States, through Pakistan, supports the anti-Western radical Gulbuddin Hekmatyar with funds and arms at the expense of other, pro-Western mujahideen commanders."

7 Department of State, *Testimony of Secretary Colin Powell before the House Appropriations Subcommittee on Foreign Operations, Export Financing and Related Programs*. February 13, 2002.

8 The Report of the Inter-Agency Working Group on Training for FY 1998 shows 51,700 foreign military and law officials trained in the United States. A report on JCET deployments for the same year lists 17,000 foreign soldiers trained abroad, for a total of 68,700 foreign police and military students. For dozens of other programs, it is not possible to quantify the number of foreign personnel receiving training, but an additional 32,000 would be a quite modest estimate for these programs.

9 Department of Defense, *Quadrennial Defense Review Report*, September 30, 2001. p.15.

10 A composite sum from the 2003 requested amounts for International Military Education and Training (IMET) and Foreign Military Financing (FMF).

11 Department of Defense news briefing, Secretary Rumsfeld and General Myers, February 8, 2002; also Oliver Teves, "Manila, U.S. Set Rules on Military Exercise," *The Washington Post*, February 14, 2002.

12 AP, "Cheney offers more military aid to Yemen," *The New York Times*, March 14, 2002; also Dan Eggen and Walter Pincus, "U.S., Yemen Step Up Anti-Terror Cooperation," *The Washington Post*, February 16, 2002.

13 Thom Shanker, "Green Beret Vanguard Arrives in the Former Soviet Georgia," *The New York Times*, April 30, 2002.

14 Elisabeth Bumiller, "Bush Vows to Aid Other Countries in War on Terror," *The New York Times*, February 12, 2002.

15 United States Institute of Peace Library—Truth Commissions: Reports: El Salvador, http://www.usip.org/library/ tc/ doc/reports/el_salvador/tc_es_03151993_toc.html; see also Saint Peter's College Library, "The Jesuit Martyrs of El Salvador: a research guide." http://www.spc.edu/library/jesuit2.html.

16 Chuck Call and Rachel Neild, "Human Rights Education and Training in US Policy Towards Latin America," from the *WOLA Report*, p. 32 (Washington Office on Latin America), 1993.

17 SOA Watch, "Pentagon Investigation Concludes that Techniques in SOA manuals were 'mistakes.'" February 21, 1997.

18 The US government provides training for an estimated 100,000 foreign military and police personnel annually; the SOA is responsible for training 600 to 800 of these foreign police and soldiers per year.

19 See Chapter 3 of this study.

20 Although Amnesty International has documented human rights violations committed by American military and police forces both in the United States and in other nations, this report focuses on foreign security officials eligible for or receiving US training. For more information on violations committed by US police and military, see "Race, Rights and Police Brutality," AI Index AMR 51/147/99 and "Afghanistan: Accountability for civilian deaths," AI Index ASA 11/022/2001.

21 Joe Braddock and Ralph Chatham, "Defense Science Board Task Force Report on Training Superiority and Training Surprise," Defense Science Board report to the Secretary of Defense, 2001.

22 Ibid.

23 Department of Defense, "DoD Dictionary of Military and Associated Terms," and NATO, "Glossary of Terms and Definitions."

24 See "Background on the Development of Rule of Law Coordination" at http://www.iawg.gov/info/reports/ fy98exrpt/appendices/appendices2/appen7ruleoflaw.html. While some fifty departments, agencies, bureaus and offices sponsor "rule of law" programs for foreign officials, this section seeks to highlight only those that involve the provision of operational police training, as opposed to judicial or legal reform, for instance.

25 See General Accounting Office, *Foreign Aid: Police Training and Assistance*, and "Background on the Development of Rule of Law Coordination."

26 Interagency Working Group on US Government-Sponsored International Exchanges & Training, Report for FY 2000, http://www.iawg.gov.

27 Department of State, "Foreign Military Training and DoD Engagement Activities of Interest Joint Report to Congress," January 2001.

28 FMS enables countries to procure US defense equipment, services and training as a total package by using national funds or US Foreign Military Financing grants.

29 According to Taw and McCoy, *RAND Note*, p. 3, over 50 percent of all Army training for foreign military students and over 80 percent of Air Force and Navy training was purchased in this way, totaling more than $200 million of training annually. By FY 1998, the amount of US military training bought by foreign militaries from around the world through FMS had jumped to $740 million. See Department of Defense and Department of State, *Foreign Military Training and DoD Engagement Activities of Interest: A Report to Congress for Fiscal Years 1998 and 1999*, p. 2 [hereafter cited as FMTR 1998-99].

30 FMTR 1998-99, Foreign Military Sales Facts as of Sept. 30, 1999; "Army School Information," http://www-satfa.monroe.army.mil/imsopage_inw.html.

31 Legislative authority provided by sections 506 and 552(c)(2) of the Foreign Assistance Act. See http://www.dsca.osd.mil/home/drawdowns.htm.

32 Department of Defense, *Security Assistance Management Manual*, paragraph 100007.

33 Interagency Working Group on US Government-Sponsored International Exchanges & Training, Report for FY 1999, Department of Defense, http://www.iawg.gov/info/reports/reports/fy99inventory/dod.html

34 FMTR 1998-99, CD ROM, "Unit Exchanges," under "Service Sponsored Activities."

35 As noted earlier, this report refers to the new institute as WHINSEC-SOA, and the school that operated until 2000 as SOA.

36 Public Law 106-398 (10 USC 2166) renames the School of the Americas and lays out its mission statement.

37 More than 1,580 US officers have attended SOA since its inception in 1946. Department of the Army, *Certifications and Report on the US Army School of the Americas*, prepared for the Committees on Appropriations of the US Congress, February 2000, p. 28.

38 General Accounting Office, *School of the Americas: US Military Training for Latin America Countries*, GAO/NSIAD-96-178, August 1996, p. 12 and see Appendix II.

39 Security Assistance Training Field Activity Internet page, http://www-satfa.monroe.army.mil/ppd/ brochure.htm.

40 Senate Foreign Relations Committee, "Foreign Policy Overview and the President's Fiscal Year 2003 Foreign Affairs Budget Request," February 5, 2002.

41 State Department, *FY 2003 Foreign Operations Budget Request*, February 4, 2002.

42 In 1998, for example, the Defense Language Institute English Language Center, located at Lackland Air Force Base, TX, provided basic English language training to at least 844 international military students (approximately one-half with grant aid and one-half cash-paying). In 1999 this number was expected to increase to 1,716 students. FMTR 1998-99, a search of the CD ROM version for English Language and "American Language" training.

43 General Accounting Office, *Security Assistance: Observations on the International Military Education and Training Program*, NSIAD-90-215BR.

44 John A. Cope, "International Military Education and Training: An Assessment," *McNair Paper*, no. 44, p. 46. Washington: National Defense University, 1995.

45 Department of Defense, *Foreign Military Training and DoD Engagement Activities of Interest*, March 1, 2000; DSCA Facts Book, September 30, 2000; Department of State, *Country Reports on Human Rights Practices*, March 4, 2002.

46 A recent study estimated that at least 13,000 Latin American soldiers alone trained with US military forces in 1999—the vast majority of them in Latin America, as opposed to in the United States. Adam Isacson and Joy Olson, *Just the Facts 2000–2001*. Washington, DC: Latin American Working Group and Center for International Policy, 1999.

47 Section 1004 of the 1991 National Defense Authorization Act.

48 In 1998 SOF made 18 deployments to Colombia, training 252 people. Such deployments also occur frequently with troops in Asian countries where illicit drugs are grown or trafficked, including Thailand. Letter from A.R. Keltz, Acting Director, Defense Security Cooperation Agency, to Sen. Jesse Helms, March 30, 1999, with attachment "DOD Engagement Activities, Unified Command Activities, Demining & Counter-Narcotics."

49 Section 1021 of the FY 2002 National Defense Authorization Act, H.R. 2586, enacted as Public Law 107-107.

50 Department of State, Bureau for International Narcotics and Law Enforcement Affairs, "International Narcotics Control Strategy Report," March 1, 2002.

51 US Central Command (CENTCOM), http://www.centcom.mil

52 FMTR 1998-99, CD ROM, "DOD Engagement Activities, National Guard Bureau."

53 According to two authorities on UN and other peacekeeping operations, "ACRI training is based on procedures from both US and intergovernmental peacekeeping doctrines. Basic soldiering skills as well as specific peacekeeping functions are taught, such as establishing checkpoints, providing perimeter security, and processing displaced persons. The importance of respecting human rights and developing and maintaining good relations with civil society is also maintained." Eric G. Berman and Katie E. Sams, *Peacekeeping in Africa: Capabilities and Culpabilities* (Geneva: UNIDIR, 2000), p. 272.

54 State Department, *FY 2003 Foreign Operations Budget Request*, February 4, 2002.

55 US Special Operations Forces, *Posture Statement 2000*, p. 15.

56 Department of Defense, 1998 *Special Operations Forces Posture Statement*, pp. 21, 91.

57 General Accounting Office, *Special Operations Forces: Opportunities to Preclude Overuse and Misuse*, GAO/NSIAD-97-85, May 1997, p. 3.

58 In other contexts, "unconventional" may refer to nuclear, chemical and biological warfare.

59 General Accounting Office, *Special Operations Forces: Opportunities to Preclude Overuse and Misuse*, GAO/NSIAD-97-85, May 1997, p. 22.

60 William C. Story, Jr., "Joint Combined Exchange Training (JCET) and Human Rights: Background and Issues for Congress," *CRS Report for Congress*, January 26, 1999, p. 4.

61 Legislative authority contained in Title 10 of the US Code, section 2011.

62 Letters from the Undersecretary of Defense to Chairmen of the House and Senate Armed Services Committees, accompanying *Report on Training of Special Operations Forces*, for FY 1997 and for FY 1998; telephone conversation with official in Special Operations and Low Intensity Conflict (SOLIC), February 2000.

63 See Dana Priest, "Chaos Tests Ties to the Pentagon," May 15, 1998; "Elite Unit Suspected of Torture," May 23, 1998; (with Doug Farah), US Force Training Troops in Colombia," May 25, 1998; "US Military Trains Foreign Troops," July 12, 1998; "Special Forces Training Review Sought," July 15, 1998; "With Military, US Makes an Overture to Algeria," November 12, 1998; "US Deepens African Military Contacts," December 13, 1998; and Doug Farah, "A Tutor to Every Army in Latin America," July 13, 1998; and Lynne Duke, "US Faces Surprise, Dilemma in Africa," July 14, 1998, *The Washington Post*.

64 Thirty-eight JCET exercises were held in Indonesia from 1992-1998, despite a ban on IMET for the country imposed by Congress in 1991. Many of the exercises took place with Kopassus, an Indonesian Special Forces unit believed to be guilty of kidnapping and torturing political dissidents.

65 Hearing before the House Subcommittee on International Operations and Human Rights: "Human Rights in Indonesia," May 7, 1998.

66 Only two of thirty US military missions to Rwanda between 1994 and August 1997 were JCET deployments; however, those were the only missions that taught combat skills. Department of Defense, *Report to Congress on US Military Activities in Rwanda 1994–August 1997*, August 19, 1997.

67 See "Memorandum for Director, Joint Staff" from Under Secretary of Defense, November 8, 1999 (document I-99/010293); "Human Rights Verification for DOD-funded Training Programs with Foreign Personnel," cable from Joint Staff, Washington, December 1999; "Guidance on Human Rights Review of DOD-funded Military Training Activities," action cable from the Secretary of State, May 1999.

68 General Accounting Office, *Foreign Aid: Police Training and Assistance*, GAO/NSIAD-92-118, March 1992.

69 Charles T. Call, "Institutional Learning within ICITAP," in Robert B. Oakley et al., eds., *Policing the New World Disorder: Peace Operations and Public Security* (Washington, DC: National Defense University, 1999); see http://www.ndu.edu/ndu/inss/books/policing/chapter9.html.

70 General Accounting Office, *Foreign Aid: Police Training and Assistance*, GAO/NSIAD-92-118.

71 Section 568 of the FY 1999 Foreign Operations Act and section 8130 of the FY 1999 DOD Appropriations Act.

72 Sources: Department of State, *Country Reports on Human Rights for 2001*, March 4, 2002; FY 2002 Foreign Operations Budget, July 2, 2001.

73 See following section of this report for further information about this program.

74 Department of State, *Congressional Budget Justification for Foreign Operations, Fiscal Year 2001*, March 15, 2000.

75 Department of State, *Congressional Budget Justification for Foreign Operations, FY 2002*, July 2, 2001.

76 The amount for 2002 was $38 million. Department of State, FY 2003 Foreign Operations Budget Request, February 4, 2002.

77 Ibid.

78 Department of State, *Budget in Brief,* from the FY 2003 Foreign Operations Budget Request, February 4, 2002.

79 FBI web page at http://www.fbi.gov/programs/academy/itp/itp.htm.

80 Kent Paterson, "Mexico's Thought Police: FBI Trained Force Allegedly Tortured Political Dissidents," *In These Times,* May 1, 2000, p. 3; see also Amnesty International USA, Urgent Action Newsletter, May and October 2000, http://www.amnestyusa.org/urgact/

81 For more information, see Amnesty International, "Who was behind the Finucane Murder?" 24 February 2000, AI Index EUR 45/35/00 and "The Killing of Human Rights Defender Rosemary Nelson," April 1, 1999, AI Index EUR 45/022/1999.

82 Section 405 of the FY 2000 Foreign Operations Appropriations, enacted as part of the Consolidated Appropriations Act for FY 2000 (Public Law 106-113).

83 http://www.iawg.gov/info/reports/fy98exrpt/appendices/inventory/agencies/doj.htm.

84 Department of Justice, International Criminal Investigative Training Assistance Program, "Year-End Review: A Compilation of Project Descriptions, 1999."

85 The Act does not specifically mention covert actions; however, section 102(d)(5) states that the agency is authorized to "perform such other functions and duties related to intelligence affecting the national security as the National Security Council may from time to time direct." This phrase has served as the legal basis for covert action and has been incorporated into presidential executive orders as authorization for such activities.

86 *The Need to Know: The Report of the 20th Century Fund Task Force on Covert Action and American Democracy* (1992), p. 85.

87 Much has been written on each of these operations. For a good overview, see John Prados, *Presidents' Secret Wars: CIA and Pentagon Covert Operations from World War II through the Persian Gulf* (Chicago: Ivan R. Dee Publishers, 1996).

88 Report of the Commission on the Roles and Capabilities of the United States Intelligence Community, p. 18.

89 Wayne Madsen, "Mercenaries in Kosovo," *The Progressive,* August 1999, p. 31.

90 See Jim Hoagland, "How CIA's Secret War on Saddam Collapsed," *The Washington Post,* June 26 1997; John Lancaster and Jonathan C. Randall, "CIA and Northern Iraq Dissidents: Little to Show for $100 Million," The Washington Post, September 15, 1996; Hugh Davis, "Secret operation that became a public disaster," *The Daily Telegraph,* September 11, 1996. Some US-based media commentators and Members of Congress have complained that the US government has not done more to train and equip anti-Saddam forces in Iraq. See, for instance, Jim Hoagland, "'Pretend' Iraq Policy," *The Washington Post,* July 2, 2000.

91 The DO maintains final approval over any military clandestine operation, so the Special Forces can only participate in covert operations at the request of, or with the permission of, the Director of Central Intelligence. Bernard C. Victory, ed., *Modernizing Intelligence: Structure and Change for the 21st Century* (Fairfax, VA: National Institute for Public Policy, Sept. 1997), pp. 87–88.

92 John Prados, who wrote an authoritative critical history of US Cold War covert actions, has argued that, for reasons of control, "if a capability for covert action is deemed essential for American security, that function would be best located within the Pentagon rather than the CIA." (Prados, p. 484.) However, the official Commission on the Roles and Capabilities of the United States Intelligence Community concluded in its final report that responsibility for paramilitary covert actions should remain with the CIA, given its "extraordinary legal authorities and an existing infrastructure that permit the secure conduct of clandestine operations." (*Preparing for*

the 21st Century: An Appraisal of US Intelligence, Report of the Commission on the Roles and Capabilities of the United States Intelligence Community, March 1, 1996, p. 19.)

93 This release of information is due largely to the efforts of private groups, like the National Security Archive, which file copious requests and lawsuits under the Freedom of Information Act. See http://www.hfni.gsehd. gwu.edu/ nsarchiv/

94 This bill was re-introduced into the 107th Congress in 2001 as H.R.1152.

95 The following companies provided training to Latin American militaries in 1998: Flight Safety International, Systems Science Corporation, Beech Aircraft Corporation, Aeroservice Aviation, Aerodyne Machine, and Allied-Signal Aerospace. Isacson and Olson, *Just the Facts 1999–2000,* pp. 168–9. Washington, DC: Latin American Working Group and Center for International Policy, 1999.

96 Legal authority contained in section 38 of the Arms Export Control Act.

97 This list includes large defense and technology multinational corporations with an array of research, development, and services, as well as small companies solely devoted to military training. All information in this report has been released publicly by the companies.

98 Kim Willenson with Nicholas Proffitt, "Persian Gulf: This Gun for Hire," *Newsweek,* February 24, 1975, p. 30. Previously, private companies had been employed for covert military and police training operations, but not through the State Department-administered commercial military sales program.

99 In addition, Science Applications International Corporation has a contract to train the Saudi Navy; Booz-Allen & Hamilton runs the Saudi Armed Forces' Staff College and helps train the recently formed Saudi Marines; and O'Gara Protective Services has been hired by the Defense Minister, Prince Sultan, to provide for the royal family's security. Ken Silverstein, "Privatizing War," The Nation, July 28, 1997.

100 Tod Robberson, "Contractors Playing Increasing Role in US Drug War," *Dallas Morning News,* February 27, 2000. In reference to the use of private contractors, General Barry McCaffrey, then-director of the US Office of National Drug Control Policy, is quoted as saying, "I am unabashedly an admirer of outsourcing." See also, Paul de la Garza and David Adams, "Military Aid...from the Private Sector," *St. Petersburg Times,* December 2, 2000.

101 See AI report "Croatia: Impunity for Killings After 'Storm'," EUR 64/04/98, August 1998 and News Releases "Three Years Since Operations Flash and Storm, Three Years of Justice and Dignity Denied," EUR 64/05/98, August 4, 1998 and "Too Soon to Hail Success in Eastern Slavonia," EUR 64/01/98, January 15, 1998.

102 For an assessment, see *Jane's Intelligence Review,* July 1998, pp. 39.

103 Letter from AIUSA to Gen. Ed Soyster (USA ret.), International Vice President, MPRI, May 1996.

104 Gerry Wallman, AIUSA Balkans Coordination Group, email correspondence January 18 and February 29, 2000.

105 Department of the Army, Inspector General, No Gun Ri Review, January 2001, pp. 5–"6.

106 Foreign Policy in Focus, "Colombia in Crisis," Vol. 5, Number 5, by Carlos Salinas, former Advocacy Director for Latin America and the Caribbean, Amnesty International USA, editors Tom Barry and Martha Honey, March 2000.

107 Section 568 of the FY 1999 Foreign Operations Act and section 8130 of the FY 1999 DoD Appropriations Act.

108 Action Memorandum for Director, Joint Staff, from Under Secretary of Defense, November 8, 1999.

109 Letter from Secretary of Defense William Cohen to Members of the House and Senate Appropriations Committees, January 21, 1998; action cable from Secretary of State to all diplomatic posts, "Screening Nominees for US-sponsored Training Programs," November 1997; joint Department of State and Department of Defense cable from the Secretary of Defense to all

Military Groups, "Guidance for Screening Candidates—US-sponsored Training Programs," December 1997.

110 Letter and information from Barbara Larkin, Assistant Secretary of State for Legislative Affairs to Senator Patrick Leahy on various embassies' implementation of the "Leahy Law," March 13, 2000.

111 The consultation requirement is relatively new. Security Assistance Act of 2000 (Public Law 106-280), Section 202.

112 Department of Defense, *Security Assistance Management Manual,* Section 100001 and Table 1000-1 (Two-Year Training Plan), February 5, 2002.

113 Bradley Graham and Vernon Loeb, "US Special Forces Troops to Train Recruits for Afghan Army," *The Washington Post,* March 26, 2002.

114 Amnesty International's current guidance for engagement in such programs is elaborated in the "Twelve Point Guide for Good Practice in the Training and Education for Human Rights of Government Officials," AI Index ACT 30/1/98, February 1998.

115 Section 202 of the Security Assistance Act of 2000 (PL 106-280).

116 Certain aspects of the database are available on the Internet, including background and basic setup. Full access is restricted. See http://disam.osd.mil/intl_training/Automation/IMSOWeb.htm

117 When asked for a list of Indonesian soldiers trained under the JCET program, the Assistant Secretary of Defense for International Security Affairs, Franklin Kramer, said his office did not have such a list ("US Lawmakers Ask for Names of Army Suspects," *Jakarta Post,* 26 July 1998, as cited in Story, *CRS Report for Congress,* p. 14). However, concerning a congressional request for information about whether a 1997 JCET event in Colombia included a particular Colombian Colonel, the Assistant Secretary of Defense for Special Operations and Low-Intensity Conflict told Amnesty USA that such records were maintained (Carlos Salinas, Acting Director for Government Affairs, Amnesty International USA, interview with Brian Sheridan, Assistant Secretary of Defense, February 2000).

118 The US Army's current law of war field manual, for example, is dated 1956, but it was substantially updated in 1976 (Department of the Army, FM 27-10, The Law of Land Warfare).

119 See Department of the Army, FM 27-14, Legal Guide for Soldiers; FM 27-1, Legal Guide for Commanders.

120 Call and Neild, *WOLA Report,* p. 5.

121 Seymour Hersch, "Overwhelming Force: What happened in the final days of the Gulf War?," *New Yorker,* May 2000, pp. 49-82.

122 Associated Press, "Bridge at No Gun Ri," by Sang-Hun Choe, Charles J. Hanley, and Martha Mendoza, September 1999.

123 Professor Douglas Linder ,"An Introduction to the My Lai Courts-Martial," University of Missouri Kansas City School of Law.

124 Peers Report, "Findings and Recommendations," located at http://www.law.umkc.edu/faculty/projects/ftrials/mylai/findings.html

125 Department of Defense, Directive 5100.77, December 9, 1998.

126 Ibid.

127 Department of Defense Directive 5410.17; see also Joint Security Assistance Training Regulation AR 12-15, "Chapter 11: Department of Defense Informational Program and Representational Activities," June 5, 2000. Available at http://web2.deskbook.osd.mil/reflib/MMULTI/001PR/011/001PR011DOC.HTM.

128 Chuck Call and Rachel Neild, "Human Rights Education and Training in US Policy Toward Latin America," Washington Office on Latin America, *WOLA Report,*1993.

129 Call and Neild, *WOLA Report,* p. 8.

130 Cope, *McNair Paper 44.*

131 "Training is the main reason IMS [international military students] come to this country. The informational program (IP) is second in importance only to training. When possible, instructors should allow IMS to be excused from class to participate in official IP functions." Message from the Director of Security Assistance Training Field Activity (SATFA) to US Army training installation commanders/school commandants, September 1995. Available at http://www-satfa.monroe.army.mil/pdd/require.htm.

132 General Accounting Office, *Security Assistance: Observations on the International Military Education and Training Program*, NSIAD-90-215BR, 1990.

133 According to a RAND Corporation report, given the experiences in El Salvador, Honduras and Thailand during the 1980s, some Members of Congress began actively to discourage internal defense and development (IDAD) training. "Congress, in a new attempt to compensate for the possible counter-democratic effects of training foreign militaries—particularly in IDAD skills— has legislated that the focus of International Military Student training must be extended to include mandatory course work in human rights, democratic values, civil control over the military and reforms of military justice systems." (Taw and McCoy, *RAND Note*, p. vi). E-IMET is thus seen by RAND authors as teaching "theoretical aspects" of IDAD (as opposed to the practical or operational), including area studies, the nature of society, the nature of insurgents, and the various roles of government in IDAD (including psychological operations and human rights initiatives). Writing in 1993, RAND reported that the JFK Special Warfare Center and School at Ft. Bragg had offered a course that deals with these subjects, but the school has been unable to give the course due to lack of participants. In effect, the report argues that Congress tried to change the content of what is being taught to developing world militaries not by altering US military doctrine, but by requiring military schools to offer some alternative course content.

134 http://www.dsca.osd.mil/eimet_default.htm.

135 Although this restriction remains in place, this may soon change. In a joint statement made by President Bush and president Megawati Soekarnoputri, the president of Indonesia, the two leaders agreed to resume regular meetings between their militaries, including multilateral exercises. "U.S. and Indonesia Pledge Cooperation: Joint Statement between the United States of America and the Republic of Indonesia," September 19, 2001.

136 Cope, *McNair Paper 44*, p. 16.

137 Department of State, Bureau of Diplomatic Security and Office of the Coordinator for Counterterrorism, *Antiterrorism Assistance Program Annual Report—Fiscal Year 2000*.

138 John Jay College for Criminal Justice, http://www.jjay.cuny.edu.

139 Call, "Institutional Learning within ICITAP," p. 13.

140 International Law Enforcement Academy, http://www.usis.hu/ilea.htm.

141 Taw and McCoy, *RAND Note*.

142 Call and Neild, *WOLA Report*, p. 32.

143 El Terrorismo de Estado en Colombia [State Terrorism in Colombia]. Brussels: Ediciones NCOS, 1992.

144 This information is cited from H.R. 732, introduced into the 106th Congress by Rep. Joe Moakley; see http://www.soaw.org for the most comprehensive lists available of former students at the SOA who have been implicated in human rights abuses.

145 Dana Priest, "US Instructed Latinos on Executions, Torture; Manuals Used 1982—91 Pentagon Reveals," *The Washington Post*, September 21, 1996, p. A1.

146 "Army Denies Use of Improper Training Manuals," *Columbus [GA] Ledger-Enquirer*, July 6, 1996.

147 See "Report on the School of the Americas," produced by the Office of Rep. Joseph Kennedy II in 1998 for the fullest description of the history and preparation of these manuals; and Lisa Haugaard, "Recently Declassified Army and CIA Manuals Used in Latin America: An Analysis of Their Content," Latin America Working Group, February 18, 1997, available at http://www.lawg.org/soafull.html. Amnesty International USA signed a letter to Secretary

of Defense William Perry and Attorney General Janet Reno in December 1996 calling for an accounting of which specific US laws, provisions of the US Military Code of Justice and provisions of international law were violated in the production, dissemination and use of these Army manuals. The letter also called on the US government to hold accountable the parties responsible for preparing these materials, and those who supervised them be held accountable for these violations. Amnesty International USA never received a reply to this letter.

148 House Amendment 723 to the Defense Authorization Bill (H.R. 4205) was offered by Rep. Moakley on May 18, 2000.

149 Public Law 106-398 (10 USC 2166) renames the School of the Americas and lays out its mission statement.

150 Title 10, United States Code, Section 2166.

151 This board has not yet convened since the opening of WHINSEC in January 2001. Of the thirteen seats on the board, five have been filled. They are: Representative Saxby Chambliss (R-Georgia), Representative Loretta Sanchez (D-California), Otto Reich from the US State Department, Major General Gary Speer from US Southern Command and General John Abrams from the US Army Training and Doctrine Command. The first meeting of the board is scheduled for early June 2002.

152 Many Army field manuals are available on the Internet at http://www.adtdl.army.mil/atdls.htm. The following manuals, however, are restricted to government officials and contractors:
FM 90-8 Counter Guerrilla Operations, August 29, 1986
FM 100-25 Doctrine for Army Special Operations Forces, August 1, 1999
FM 31-20 Doctrine for Special Forces Operations, April 20, 1990
FM 31-20-3 Foreign Internal Defense Tactics, Techniques and Procedures for Special Forces, September 20, 1994
FM 7-85 Ranger Unit Operations, June 9, 1987
FM 23-9 M16A1 and M16A2 Rifle Marksmanship, July 3, 1989
FM 33-1 Psychological Operations, February 18, 1993
FM 33-1-1 Psychological Operations Techniques and Procedures, May 5, 1994

153 FM 100-20 Military Operations in Low Intensity Conflict, December 5, 1990

154 WHINSEC web site, http://www-benning.army.mil/whisc; also US Army, "Army School Information," http://www-satfa.monroe.army.mil/imsopage_inw.html.

155 Department of the Army, *Certifications and Report on the US Army School of the Americas*, prepared for the Committees on Appropriations of the US Congress, February 2000, p. 10.

156 Department of Defense, *Expanded IMET Handbook*, November 2001.

157 WHINSEC web site.

158 Letter from US Army Major Tony Raimondo, Chief of the Human Rights and International Law Division at WHINSEC-SOA, July 20, 2001.

159 The only exception to this comes under the US Southern Command's Operational Overview, which states that USSOUTHCOM "ensures that human rights training and guidance are incorporated into all USSOUTHCOM-sponsored military-to-military contact programs."

160 Letter from Undersecretary of Defense Walter Slocombe to Chairman, House/Senate Armed Services Committee, April 1, 1999.

161 Michael McClintock asks in Instruments of Statecraft, "Is it reasonable to expect that forces specialized in the tactics of terror can play a convincing role in human rights training?" He notes that in the 1980s, a civilian legal consultant to the Pentagon, William O'Brien, argued that the brief duration, specific targeting and urgency of special operations justify "exceptions to the normal moral and legal constraints" on military actions. McClintock, *Instruments of Statecraft*, p. 423.

162 When Amnesty International USA first called USSOCOM public affairs to inquire about the existence of any relevant pre- or post-deployment human rights guidance, the organization was

told there was none. Public affairs called back shortly thereafter to say that there was indeed a policy.

163 Call and Neild, *WOLA Report*, p. 15.

164 Department of Defense, US Southern Command, "Administration: Human Rights Policy and Procedures," SC Regulation 1-20, July 1, 1998.

165 Summary Report to Congress on US Military Activities in Rwanda, 1994–August 1997, updated June 15, 1998, http://www.defenselink.mil/pubs/rwanda/summary.html, printed January 24, 2000.

166 "Alarming Resurgence of Killings," AI Index AFR 47/13/96, 1996. See also "Human Rights Violations by the Rwandan Government Security Forces," documentation for the Leahy Amendment Implementation project, July 6, 1998, which includes various Amnesty International documents on human rights violations by the RPA.

167 Rep Smith reiterated, "So, you would be convinced that US sources would not be used, or training, or diverted in any way to help rebels who might be committing massacres?" Kern replied, "I do not see any way that could possibly happen." *Refugees in Eastern Zaire and Rwanda*, Hearing of the Subcommittee on International Operations and Human Rights, House Committee on International Relations, December 4, 1996, p. 19.

168 See memoranda from Capt. Joel B. Rieman, leader of the 3rd Army Special Forces Group training detachment involved in "Falcon Gorilla," to his chain of command, dated May 29 and June 3, 1996.

169 Summary Report to Congress on US Military Activities in Rwanda, 1994-August 1997, updated June 15, 1998, http://www.defenselink.mil/pubs/rwanda/summary.html, printed January 24, 2000.

170 Lynne Duke, "Africans Use Training in Unexpected Ways," *The Washington Post*, July 14, 1998, p. A1.

171 UN High Commissioner for Human Rights, UN Human Rights Field Operation in Rwanda, "Deterioration of the Security and Human Rights Situation in Ruhengeri Prefecture, Including Killings of Civilians during Military Operations, May-June 1997," status report as of August 7, 1997 at http://www.unhchr.ch/html/ menu2/5/ rwanda/rwa_sr8.htm. According to representatives of the Rwandan government cited in this report, during May-June 200-300 civilians were killed during military operations; 1,800 members of armed groups were killed during confrontations; and 90 RPA soldiers, including four officers, were killed.

172 Human Rights Watch, "Eastern Congo Ravaged: Killing Civilians and Silencing Protest," vol. 12, no. 3(A), May 2000, p. 3.

173 Amnesty International, "Rwanda: The hidden violence: 'disappearances' and killings continue," AI Index AFR 47/023/1998, June 23, 1998.

174 Jill Jolliffe, "Back from the dead," East Timor Action Network. Originally in the *Sydney Morning Herald*, June 19, 1999; see also http://www.etan.org, "Santa Cruz massacre."

175 Allan Nairn, "Indonesia's Killers," *The Nation*, March 30, 1998, pp. 6–7.

176 Letter from John J. Hamre, Deputy Secretary of Defense, to Rep. Lane Evans, July 15, 1998.

177 Ibid.

178 The individual was Col. Slamat Disabutar, who had attended the US Army Command and General Staff College at Ft. Leavenworth in 1992 and the US Army Ranger school. See Amnesty International USA's, "Human Rights Violations by the Indonesian Security Forces: Notes and Documentation for the Leahy Amendment Implementation Project," July 16, 1998.

179 Rajiv Chandrasekaran, "US Resumes Training Indonesian Army Officers," *The Washington Post*, February 19, 2000, p. A21.

180 CBS 60 Minutes II, "The Secret War," broadcast October 1999.

181 International Women's Media Foundation, "A Spirit Uncrushed," October 2001; see also *Amnesty International Annual Report 2001*.

182 American Embassy Bogota, "Narcotics Activity Report," monthly report from January 1993–February 1994.

183 Letter from twenty-four members of Congress to President Clinton, organized by Rep. Janice D. Schakowsky, December 2000.

184 Santa Fe de Bogota Emisoras Caracol Network, July 22, 1997, in FBIS-LAT-97-203

185 Ignacio Gomez, "The Risks of US Aid," *El Espectador,* February 27, 2000.

186 Letter from Brian Sheridan, Assistant Secretary of Defense for Special Operations and Low-Intensity Conflict to Sen. Patrick Leahy, May 22, 2000.

187 Scott Wilson, "Colombian General Convicted in Killings," *The Washington Post,* February 14, 2001, p. A19.

188 Memorandum by Col. Warren D. Hall III, Staff Judge Advocate, to CINC SOUTHCOM, April 8, 1994.

189 US Department of State, "FY 2003 Foreign Operations Budget Request," February 4, 2002.